Leveled Text-Dependent Question Stems

Reread the ______ paragraph. How does this paragraph relate to the main idea of the text?

Why does the author use the word/phrase ______ to describe ______?

What are the key details in the ______ paragraph?

Author
Debra Housel, M.S.Ed.

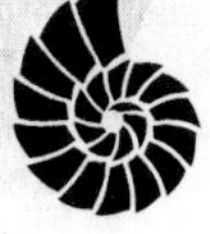

SHELL EDUCATION

Publishing Credits

Corinne Burton, M.A.Ed., *President*; Emily R. Smith, M.A.Ed., *Editorial Director*; Grace Alba Le, *Multimedia Designer*; Stephanie Bernard, *Assistant Editor*; Don Tran, *Production Artist*; Amber Goff, *Editorial Assistant*

Shell Education
5301 Oceanus Drive
Huntington Beach, CA 92649-1030
http://www.shelleducation.com

ISBN 978-1-4258-1475-5

Table of Contents

Introduction 4
- What Are Text-Dependent Questions? 4
- Leveled Text-Dependent Questions 4
- Literacy Skill Descriptions 5
- How to Use This Book 9

Understanding Main Idea and Theme 10

Identifying Key Details 22

Summarizing 34

Using Text Features 46

Identifying the Setting 58

Understanding the Plot 70

Analyzing Characters 82

Analyzing Text Structure 94

Identifying Point of View 106

Recognizing Figurative Language 118

Identifying Tone 130

Making Inferences 142

Answer Key 154

Image Credits 160

What Are Text-Dependent Questions?

From literary novels and dramas, to textbooks, newspaper articles, statistical reports, and websites, texts vary in content and style. Regardless of the format, students must be able to decode and comprehend the contents of the texts to learn from the material. Text-dependent questions increase students' understanding through in-depth examinations of particular aspects of the texts. They guide students to examine specific portions of the texts and then provide evidence for their answers. Unlike other types of questions, text-dependent questions rely solely on the text so that students may not necessarily need to access significant background knowledge or include outside information.

Text-dependent questions facilitate the comprehension of text on a variety of levels. On the most specific level, these questions help students analyze words and sentences within the text to determine the specific meaning and connotations of particular words and phrases. Text-dependent questions also enable students to study broader concepts, such as text structure and point of view. They aid students in their study of the individuals, settings, and sequences of events in a text and also provide a means for investigating the presence of other types of media within the writing (e.g., drawings, illustrations, graphs, tables). These questions offer an effective tool for helping students analyze the overarching themes, concepts, arguments, and claims presented in texts. Text-dependent questions help students build their abilities to compare multiple texts to each other on a variety of topics. Through thoughtful design and sequencing, text-dependent questions can be tailored to meet many specific educational standards and learning objectives while still maintaining a direct connection to the text.

Leveled Text-Dependent Questions

Leveling text-dependent questions helps teachers differentiate content to allow all students access to the concepts being explored. While the text-dependent question stems are written at a variety of levels, each level remains strong in focusing on the content and vocabulary presented in the texts. Teachers can focus on the same content standard or objective for the whole class, but individual students can access the texts at their individual instructional levels rather than at their frustration levels.

Teachers can also use the text-dependent questions as a scaffold for teaching students. At the beginning of the year, students at the lowest reading levels may need focused teacher guidance as they respond to the questions. As the year progresses, teachers can begin giving students multiple levels of the same questions to aid them in improving their comprehension independently. By scaffolding the content in this way, teachers can support students as they move up through the thinking levels.

Note—Throughout this book, the term *text* is used in the leveled text-dependent question stems to refer to informational texts, narrative nonfiction texts, stories, passages, plays, poems, and so on. When asking the questions to students, teachers should substitute the specific type of text for that word. The examples illustrate how to do this.

Literacy Skill Descriptions

Understanding the Main Idea and Theme

The ability to identify the main idea or theme is crucial to the construction of meaning when reading texts.

Literature

With the exception of fables, identifying the theme of a story is a critical thinking skill that requires the reader to make an inference based on the events. The theme is the "big idea" that extends beyond the level of the story.

Informational Texts

Students look for a main idea statement and the key details that support it. If there is no main idea stated, students must be able to infer the main idea based on the details presented.

Identifying Key Details

Key details are stated. The task for the reader is to distinguish between key and minor details that make a text interesting and vivid versus key details that provide supporting information. This requires the reader to make connections within the content to find the overarching ideas.

Literature

Students first determine the theme of the story, which is typically only stated in fables. The theme is the "big idea," or a life lesson that applies to the world beyond the story. Once the theme has been identified, students then choose the details that support it.

Informational Texts

Students first identify the main idea and then determine which details support it. If the main idea is unstated, students must infer the main idea and then decide which details support it.

Summarizing

When students know how to summarize, their overall comprehension improves. Summarizing requires pulling the main ideas and important details from the overall text and putting them in a logical order. Encourage students to summarize both during and after reading.

Literature

Students review the title; chapter titles; illustrations; main events in the beginning, middle, and end; central characters; key details; the tone; and the structure of the text to summarize.

Informational Texts

Students use text features such as titles, chapter titles, bold words, side headings, captions, and diagrams to determine what to include in summaries.

Literacy Skill Descriptions *(cont.)*

Using Text Features

In addition to reading the main body of a text, good readers use headings, captions, diagrams, and other text features to navigate and fully comprehend the text. Referencing these features throughout the reading process helps students to understand, remember, comprehend, and make predictions about the content.

Literature	Informational Texts
Students reference the title, cover illustration, back-cover summary, table of contents, chapter titles, illustrations, and captions to understand a novel, poem, or drama.	Students use the table of contents, chapters, glossary, index, titles, headings, labels, captions, photographs, sketches, diagrams, charts, graphs, maps, tables, figures, time lines, footnotes, cross-sections, insets, sidebars, bold words, and graphic organizers to increase comprehension of informational texts.

Identifying the Setting

When readers can answer the question "What is this place like?" it heightens their ability to discern the elements of setting. When they find specific examples in the text that lead them to their understanding of time, place, and environment, they deepen their understanding of the text.

Literature	Nonfiction Narratives
Students study details in the text to determine the three elements of setting: time, place, and overall environment.	Understanding the setting is important to comprehending nonfiction narratives. Students can pick up clues about the time period, location, and environment from the wording in the text.

Understanding the Plot

If an author uses flashbacks, flash-forwards, and multiple narrators and storylines, a novel's plot is not always a straightforward algorithm. Therefore, learning to ascertain which events are occurring and in what order or in relationship to each other is an important part of comprehension for any reader.

Literature	Nonfiction Narrative
Students identify the conflict, which is the primary problem from which all events stem in the story. They follow the rising action to its climax, or turning point, and then the story is quickly resolved, or ended. If there are multiple plots within the novel, there will be multiple climaxes and resolutions before the final one.	Some informational texts are written in a story format to draw in the reader and increase interest. In general, there is one plot and few, if any, plot devices such as flashbacks. Multiple narrators may be used to help the reader understand varying viewpoints in informational texts.

Literacy Skill Descriptions *(cont.)*

Analyzing Characters

The ability to analyze characters or people based on their words and actions not only improves readers' comprehension, but it also helps students to make accurate predictions about what people may do or say in future situations. The ability to make such predictions is a critical thinking skill that underlies the ability to draw conclusions or make inferences.

Literature

Writers rarely come right out and state what a character is like. Students must look at each character's actions or speech to uncover the clues to ascertain that character's personality traits.

Informational Texts

In informational texts, character analysis is most often done in biographies and autobiographies. The ability to identify and evaluate the central person's motivation helps students to comprehend the characters' actions.

Analyzing Text Structure

Students need to be aware of the way text structure influences meaning and how authors use the structure of a text to evoke a desired effect in the reader. Students should understand how ideas in a text relate to one another and how information is organized. Readers who understand the structure of a text can use this knowledge to make predictions and understand the author's purpose more easily.

Literature

Students identify the genre and structure of a literary text, noting whether a piece is a mystery, poem, drama, etc. Students analyze how components of a text such as paragraphs, chapters, scenes, and stanzas relate to each other.

Informational Texts

Students recognize a variety of nonfiction text types such as compare and contrast, cause and effect, and problem and solution. Students understand how each part of a text contributes to the whole.

Identifying Point of View

Students consider people's or characters' thoughts, speech, and actions to determine viewpoints. Often students will identify with one character or person and reject or dislike others based on how closely students relate to the views.

Literature

Authors will often create intriguing characters that have various viewpoints. Readers identify with or reject different characters' stances. It is why there are heroes and villains in most literature. If the story is told through the eyes of one character, the remaining characters' viewpoints must be inferred from their speech and behavior.

Informational Texts

Students identify the author's viewpoint. Then they look for the word choices the author makes in stating that viewpoint. They search for clues or facts that support the author's stance. Authors write informational texts to inform, to entertain, or to persuade. The author's viewpoint in informational texts guides the reader to look for the facts on which it rests.

Literacy Skill Descriptions *(cont.)*

Recognizing Figurative Language

Figurative language is one thing that makes a written work interesting. It helps the reader to draw comparisons between the text and things they may already know. Commonly used figurative language forms are simile, metaphor, personification, and hyperbole.

Literature	Informational Texts
Students study the words used in a text to identify similes, metaphors, personification, and exaggeration (hyperbole). Once identified, figurative language can be analyzed for its deeper meanings.	Students recognize figurative language use and then make judgments regarding whether it is used appropriately in informational text. For example, if exaggeration occurs in nonfiction, is it still legitimate to call it a report, or is it actually an editorial?

Identifying Tone

Tone is the writer's attitude toward his or her written piece, but it is not directly stated. The reader infers the tone in order to determine how to react to the piece. For example, in a ghost story, the tone may be fear, and the reader realizes that the writer wants him or her to feel afraid.

Literature	Informational Texts
Students need to infer the tone by searching for clues. Since the tone affects the readers' mood, one question to ask is, "How does reading this make me feel?" Follow with the question, "What words or events occurred that prompted me to feel that way?" in order to find the phrases or events that create the tone.	Reporters try to state the facts without tone in most newspapers and online accounts. Students need to assess the writer's word choices for connotations to determine if the text has a specific tone and if so, what that tone is and if it is appropriate to use in the text.

Making Inferences

Good readers have the ability to make inferences and draw conclusions. This skill is vital to genuine comprehension of any text. Without the ability to infer, readers are merely word calling. The more experience a reader has in drawing conclusions, the more accurate his or her predictions are likely to be.

Literature	Informational Texts
Students analyze each character's thoughts and behaviors to learn who that person really is. They consider the setting (context) and the plot in order to make inferences and other predictions about what will happen next.	Students must look for the "unspoken truths" in informational texts in order to get the complete message. They move from simply reading facts that are directly stated to thinking about why the facts exist.

How to Use This Book

Skill Overview—Each skill is defined on the first page of its section. This will remind teachers what the skill is and how to introduce it to students.

Complexity—The text-dependent question stems in this book are differentiated to four complexity levels. The levels roughly correlate to four grade ranges as follows:

- ☆ grades K–1
- ○ grades 2–4
- □ grades 5–8
- △ grades 9–12

Implementing the Question Stems—The second page of each section contains an example question stem differentiated to all four complexity levels and for both literature and informational text. This is a great way for teachers to see a model of how the leveled text-dependent questions can be used with their students. Throughout the section, there are also sample student pages with passages and leveled questions using the question stems.

Question Stems—Each of the 12 sections includes 10 question stems differentiated to four complexity levels for a total of 480 questions in the book. Along with a chart showing the 10 question stems, each complexity level also includes a leveled passage with sample text-dependent questions.

K–12 Question Stems Vertical Alignment—The final two pages in each section include the leveled text-dependent question stems in one chart. This way, teachers can use just these two pages to differentiate the text-dependent questions they are asking their students.

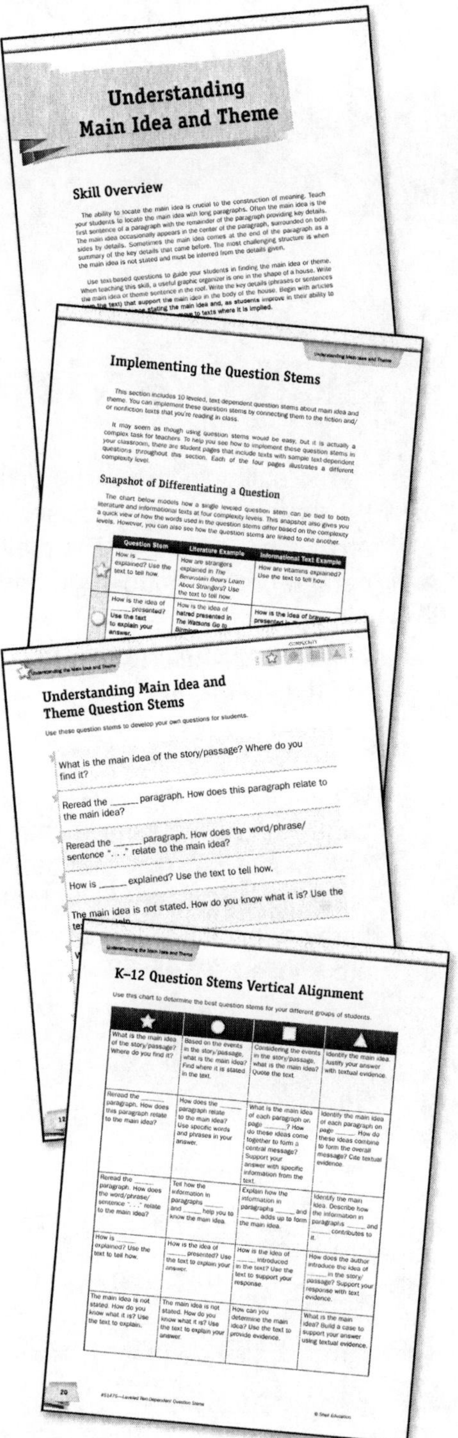

Understanding Main Idea and Theme

Skill Overview

The ability to locate the main idea is crucial to the construction of meaning. Teach your students to locate the main idea with long paragraphs. Often the main idea is the first sentence of a paragraph with the remainder of the paragraph providing key details. The main idea occasionally appears in the center of the paragraph, surrounded on both sides by details. Sometimes the main idea comes at the end of the paragraph as a summary of the key details that came before. The most challenging structure is when the main idea is not stated and must be inferred from the details given.

Use text-based questions to guide your students in finding the main idea or theme. When teaching this skill, a useful graphic organizer is one in the shape of a house. Write the main idea or theme sentence in the roof. Write the key details (phrases or sentences from the text) that support the main idea in the body of the house. Begin with articles ... stating the main idea and, as students improve in their ability to ... to texts where it is implied.

Implementing the Question Stems

This section includes 10 leveled, text dependent question stems about main idea and theme. You can implement these question stems by connecting them to the fiction and/or nonfiction texts that you're reading in class.

It may seem as though using question stems would be easy, but it is actually a complex task for teachers. To help you see how to implement these question stems in your classroom, there are student pages that include texts with sample text-dependent questions throughout this section. Each of the four pages illustrates a different complexity level.

Snapshot of Differentiating a Question

The chart below models how a single leveled question stem can be tied to both literature and informational texts at four complexity levels. This snapshot also gives you a quick view of how the words used in the question stems differ based on the complexity levels. However, you can also see how the question stems are linked to one another.

	Question Stem	Literature Example	Informational Text Example
☆	How is ______ explained? Use the text to tell how.	How are strangers explained in *The Berenstain Bears Learn About Strangers*? Use the text to tell how.	How are vitamins explained? Use the text to tell how.
○	How is the idea of ______ presented? Use the text to explain your answer.	How is the idea of hatred presented in *The Watsons Go to Birmin...*	How is the idea of bravery presented...

Understanding Main Idea and Theme Question Stems

Use these question stems to develop your own questions for students.

What is the main idea of the story/passage? Where do you find it?

Reread the ______ paragraph. How does this paragraph relate to the main idea?

Reread the ______ paragraph. How does the word/phrase/sentence "..." relate to the main idea?

How is ______ explained? Use the text to tell how.

The main idea is not stated. How do you know what it is? Use the ...

K–12 Question Stems Vertical Alignment

Use this chart to determine the best question stems for your different groups of students.

☆	○	□	△
What is the main idea of the story/passage? Where do you find it?	Based on the events in the story/passage, what is the main idea? Find where it is stated in the text.	Considering the events in the story/passage, what is the main idea? Quote the text.	Identify the main idea. Justify your answer with textual evidence.
Reread the ______ paragraph. How does this paragraph relate to the main idea?	How does the ______ paragraph relate to the main idea? Use specific words and phrases in your answer.	What is the main idea of each paragraph on page ______? How do these ideas come together to form a central message? Support your answer with specific information from the text.	Identify the main idea of each paragraph on page ______. How do these ideas combine to form the overall message? Cite textual evidence.
Reread the ______ paragraph. How does the word/phrase/sentence "..." relate to the main idea?	Tell how the information in paragraphs ______ and ______ help you to know the main idea.	Explain how the information in paragraphs ______ and ______ adds up to form the main idea.	Identify the main idea. Describe how the information in paragraphs ______ and ______ contributes to it.
How is ______ explained? Use the text to tell how.	How is the idea of ______ presented? Use the text to explain your answer.	How is the idea of ______ introduced in the text? Use the text to support your response.	How does the author introduce the idea of ______ in the story/passage? Support your response with text evidence.
The main idea is not stated. How do you know what it is? Use the text to explain.	The main idea is not stated. How do you know what it is? Use the text to explain your answer.	How can you determine the main idea? Use the text to provide evidence.	What is the main idea? Build a case to support your answer using textual evidence.

20 #51475—Leveled Text-Dependent Question Stems © Shell Education

Understanding Main Idea and Theme

Skill Overview

The ability to locate the main idea is crucial to the construction of meaning. Often the main idea is the first sentence of a paragraph, with the remainder of the paragraph providing key details. The main idea occasionally appears in the center of the paragraph, surrounded on both sides by details. Sometimes the main idea comes at the end of the paragraph as a summary of the key details that came before. The most challenging structure is when the main idea is not stated and must be inferred from the details given.

Use text-based questions to guide your students in finding the main idea or theme. When teaching this skill, a useful graphic organizer is one in the shape of a house. Write the main idea or theme sentence in the roof. Write the key details (phrases or sentences from the text) that support the main idea in the body of the house. When teaching, begin with texts that clearly state the main idea and, as students improve in their abilities to identify main ideas or themes, move to texts where main ideas are implied.

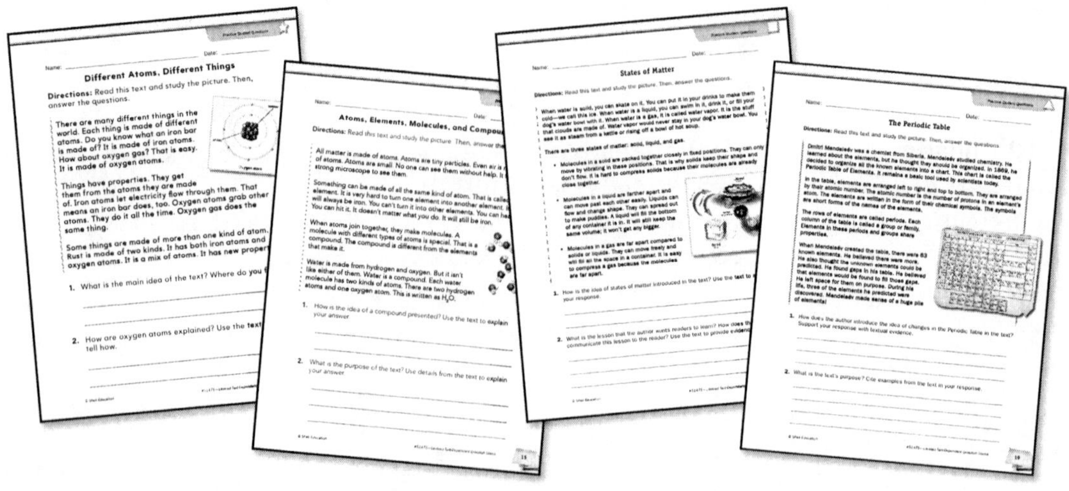

Implementing the Question Stems

This section includes 10 leveled, text-dependent question stems about main idea and theme. You can implement these question stems by connecting them to the fiction passages and/or nonfiction texts that you are reading in class.

It may seem as though using question stems would be easy, but it can be a complex task for teachers. To help you see how to implement these question stems in your classroom, this section includes student pages containing texts with sample text-dependent questions. Each of the four student pages illustrates a different complexity level.

Snapshot of Differentiating a Question

The chart below models how a single leveled question stem can be tied to both literature passages and informational texts at four complexity levels. This snapshot also gives you a quick view of how the question stems differ based on the complexity levels. However, you can also see how the question stems link to one another.

	Question Stem	Literature Example	Informational Text Example
☆	How is ______ explained? Use the text to tell how.	How are strangers explained in *The Berenstain Bears Learn About Strangers*? Use the book to tell how.	How are vitamins explained? Use the text to tell how.
○	How is the idea of ______ presented? Use the text to explain your answer.	How is the idea of hatred presented in *The Watsons Go to Birmingham—1963*? Use the novel to explain your answer.	How is the idea of bravery presented in *The Angel of Marye's Heights*? Use the text to explain your answer.
□	How is the idea of ______ introduced in the text? Use the text to support your response.	How is the idea of responsibility introduced in *On My Honor*? Use the novel to support your response.	How is the idea of cyberbullying introduced in the text? Use the text to support your response.
△	How does the author introduce the idea of ______ in the text? Support your response with textual evidence.	How does the author introduce the idea of immorality in *The Portrait of Dorian Gray*? Support your response with textual evidence.	How does the author introduce the idea of environmental conservation in the magazine article? Support your response with textual evidence.

COMPLEXITY

LOW

Understanding Main Idea and Theme Question Stems

Use these question stems to develop your own questions for students.

What is the main idea of the text? Where do you find it?

Reread the ______ paragraph/sentence. How does this paragraph/sentence relate to the main idea?

Reread the ______ paragraph. How does the word/phrase/sentence ". . ." relate to the main idea?

How is ______ explained? Use the text to tell how.

The main idea is not stated. How do you know what it is? Use the text to explain.

What is the theme? How do you know?

Is there more than one theme in the text? How do you know?

How do the events add up to create the theme? Explain.

What is the moral of the text? How do you know?

Why does the author write this text? How do you know?

Name: ______________________ Date: ______________

Different Atoms, Different Things

Directions: Read this text and study the picture. Then, answer the questions.

neutron
electron
proton
Oxygen atom

There are many different things in the world. Each thing is made of different atoms. Do you know what an iron bar is made of? It is made of iron atoms. How about oxygen gas? That is easy. It is made of oxygen atoms.

Things have properties. They get them from the atoms they are made of. Iron atoms let electricity flow through them. That means an iron bar does, too. Oxygen atoms grab other atoms. They do it all the time. Oxygen gas does the same thing.

Some things are made of more than one kind of atom. Rust is made of two kinds. It has both iron atoms and oxygen atoms. It is a mix of atoms. It has new properties.

1. What is the main idea of the text? Where do you find it?

____

____

2. How are oxygen atoms explained? Use the text to tell how.

____

____

COMPLEXITY

LOW

Understanding Main Idea and Theme Question Stems

Use these question stems to develop your own questions for students.

Based on the events in the text, what is the main idea? Find where it is stated in the text.

How does the ______ paragraph/sentence relate to the main idea? Use specific words and phrases in your answer.

Tell how the information in paragraphs/sentences ______ and ______ help you to understand the main idea.

How is the idea of ______ presented? Use the text to explain your answer.

The main idea is not stated. How do you know what it is? Use the text to explain your answer.

What is the theme of the text? Use details from the text to support your answer.

Name the multiple themes in the text. How do they work together? Give specific details from the text.

Describe how the events on page ______ relate to the theme. Give proof from the text to support this idea.

What is the text's lesson? How does the author make that clear to the reader? Give examples from the text.

What is the purpose of the text? Use details from the text to explain your answer.

Name: ______________________________ Date: ____________

Atoms, Elements, Molecules, and Compounds

Directions: Read this text and study the picture. Then, answer the questions.

All matter is made of atoms. Atoms are tiny particles. Even air is made of atoms. Atoms are small. No one can see them without help. It takes a strong microscope to see them.

Something can be made of all the same kind of atom. That is called an element. It is very hard to turn one element into another element. Iron will always be iron. You can't turn it into other elements. You can heat it. You can hit it. It doesn't matter what you do. It will still be iron.

When atoms join together, they make molecules. A molecule with different types of atoms is special. That is a compound. The compound is different from the elements that make it.

Water is made from hydrogen and oxygen. But it isn't like either of them. Water is a compound. Each water molecule has two kinds of atoms. There are two hydrogen atoms and one oxygen atom. This is written as H_2O.

1. How is the idea of a compound presented? Use the text to explain your answer.

____

____

2. What is the purpose of the text? Use details from the text to explain your answer.

____

____

____

COMPLEXITY

Understanding Main Idea and Theme Question Stems

Use these question stems to develop your own questions for students.

Considering the events in the text, what is the main idea? Quote the text in your answer.

What is the main idea of each paragraph on page ______? How do these ideas come together to form a central message? Support your answer with specific information from the text.

Explain how the information in paragraphs ______ and ______ adds up to form the main idea.

How is the idea of ______ introduced in the text? Use the text to support your response.

How can you determine the main idea? Use the text to provide evidence.

What is the theme of the text? Give specific examples from the text to support your answer.

What are the multiple themes in the text? How do these themes combine in the text? Include specific details from the text in your answer.

Explain how the events on page ______ relate to the theme of the text. What evidence from the text supports this idea?

What is the lesson that the author wants readers to learn? How does the author communicate this lesson to the reader? Use the text to provide evidence.

What was the author's purpose in writing this text? Include examples from the text to support your answer.

Name: ______________________________ Date: ______________

States of Matter

Directions: Read this text and study the picture. Then, answer the questions.

When water is solid, you can skate on it. You can put it in your drinks to make them cold—we call this ice. When water is a liquid, you can swim in it, drink it, or fill your dog's water bowl with it. When water is a gas, it is called water vapor. It is the stuff that clouds are made of. Water vapor would never stay in your dog's water bowl. You see it as steam from a kettle or rising off a bowl of hot soup.

There are three states of matter: solid, liquid, and gas.

- Molecules in a solid are packed together closely in fixed positions. They can only move by vibrating in these positions. That is why solids keep their shape and don't flow. It is hard to compress solids because their molecules are already close together.
- Molecules in a liquid are farther apart and can move past each other easily. Liquids can flow and change shape. They can spread out to make puddles. A liquid will fill the bottom of any container it is in. It will still keep the same volume; it won't get any bigger.
- Molecules in a gas are far apart compared to solids or liquids. They can move freely and will fill all the space in a container. It is easy to compress a gas because the molecules are far apart.

1. How is the idea of states of matter introduced in the text? Use the text to support your response.

____

____

2. What is the lesson that the author wants readers to learn? How does the author communicate this lesson to the reader? Use the text to provide evidence.

____

____

____

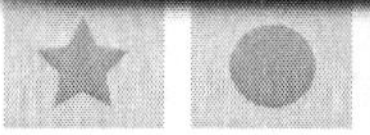

Understanding Main Idea and Theme Question Stems

Use these question stems to develop your own questions for students.

Identify the main idea. Justify your answer with textual evidence.

Identify the main idea of each paragraph on page _____. How do these ideas combine to form the overall message? Cite textual evidence.

Identify the main idea. Describe how the information in paragraphs _____ and _____ contributes to it.

How does the author introduce the idea of _____ in the text? Support your response with textual evidence.

What is the main idea? Build a case to support your answer using textual evidence.

What is the text's theme? Cite textual evidence to illustrate your response.

Describe the multiple themes in the text. How are these themes interwoven throughout the text? Justify your answer with specific details from the text.

Explain how the series of events on page _____ contributes to the overall theme. Justify your answer with evidence from the text.

What is the message that the author wants readers to take away from the text? How does the author communicate this information to the reader? Cite textual evidence in your answer.

What is the text's purpose? Cite examples from the text in your response.

Name: ______________________________ Date: ______________

The Periodic Table

Directions: Read this text and study the picture. Then, answer the questions.

Dmitri Mendeleév was a chemist from Siberia. Mendeleév studied chemistry. He learned about the elements, but he thought they should be organized. In 1869, he decided to organize all the known elements into a chart. This chart is called the Periodic Table of Elements. It remains a basic tool used by scientists today.

In the table, elements are arranged left to right and top to bottom. They are arranged by their atomic number. The atomic numbers is the number of protons in an element's atom. The elements are written in the forms of their chemical symbols. The symbols are short forms of the names of the elements.

The rows of elements are called periods. Each column of the table is called a group or family. Elements in these periods and groups share properties.

When Mendeleév created the table, there were 63 known elements. He believed there were more. He also thought the unknown elements could be predicted. He found gaps in his table. He believed that elements would be found to fill those gaps. He left space for them on purpose. During his life, three of the elements he predicted were discovered. Mendeleév made sense of a huge pile of elements!

1. How does the author introduce the idea of changes in the Periodic Table in the text? Support your response with textual evidence.

____

____

____

2. What is the text's purpose? Cite examples from the text in your response.

____

____

____

____

Understanding Main Idea and Theme K–12 Alignment

Use this chart to determine the best question stems for your different groups of students.

☆	○	□	△
What is the main idea of the text? Where do you find it?	Based on the events in the text, what is the main idea? Find where it is stated in the text.	Considering the events in the text, what is the main idea? Quote the text in your answer.	Identify the main idea. Justify your answer with textual evidence.
Reread the ______ paragraph/sentence. How does this paragraph relate to the main idea?	How does the ______ paragraph/sentence relate to the main idea? Use specific words and phrases in your answer.	What is the main idea of each paragraph on page ______? How do these ideas come together to form a central message? Support your answer with specific information from the text.	Identify the main idea of each paragraph on page ______. How do these ideas combine to form the overall message? Cite textual evidence.
Reread the ______ paragraph/sentence. How does the word/phrase/sentence ". . ." relate to the main idea?	Tell how the information in paragraphs/sentences ______ and ______ help you to understand the main idea.	Explain how the information in paragraphs ______ and ______ adds up to form the main idea.	Identify the main idea. Describe how the information in paragraphs ______ and ______ contributes to it.
How is ______ explained? Use the text to tell how.	How is the idea of ______ presented? Use the text to explain your answer.	How is the idea of ______ introduced in the text? Use the text to support your response.	How does the author introduce the idea of ______ in the text? Support your response with textual evidence.
The main idea is not stated. How do you know what it is? Use the text to explain.	The main idea is not stated. How do you know what it is? Use the text to explain your answer.	How can you determine the main idea? Use the text to provide evidence.	What is the main idea? Build a case to support your answer using textual evidence.

Understanding Main Idea and Theme K–12 Alignment *(cont.)*

☆	○	□	△
What is the theme? How do you know?	What is the theme of the text? Use details from the text to support your answer.	What is the theme of the text? Give specific examples from the text to support your answer.	What is the text's theme? Cite textual evidence to illustrate your response.
Is there more than one theme in the text? How do you know?	Name the multiple themes in the text. How do they work together? Give specific details from the text.	What are the multiple themes in the text? How do these themes combine in the text? Include specific details from the text in your answer.	Describe the multiple themes in the text. How are these themes interwoven throughout the text? Justify your answer with specific details from the text.
How do the events add up to create the theme? Explain.	Describe how the events on page ______ relate to the theme. Give proof from the text to support this idea.	Explain how the events on page ______ relate to the theme of the text. What evidence from the text supports this idea?	Explain how the series of events on page ______ contribute to the overall theme. Justify your answer with evidence from the text.
What is the moral of the text? How do you know?	What is the text's lesson? How does the author make that clear to the reader? Give examples from the text.	What is the lesson that the author wants readers to learn? How does the author communicate this lesson to the reader? Use the text to provide evidence.	What is the message that the author wants readers to take away from the text? How does the author communicate this information to the reader? Cite textual evidence in your answer.
Why does the author write this text? How do you know?	What is the purpose of the text? Use details from the text to explain your answer.	What was the author's purpose in writing this text? Include examples from the text to support your answer.	What is the text's purpose? Cite examples from the text in your response.

Identifying Key Details

Skill Overview

Key details are stated. This means that you need to teach your students to locate them as sentences or phrases. Teach your students to first locate the main idea of a text and then determine which ideas support it. If the main idea is only implied, then finding the key details must happen first.

Use text-based questions to guide your students in locating key details. For different texts, you can choose questions that help students to focus on the sequence, characters, plot, or author's purpose. As an added benefit, helping your students to identify why an author includes specific details will strengthen their writing skills.

Just as a main idea is supported by key details, blocks must support the top of a pyramid. Students can graphically represent the main idea and key details using a pyramid graphic organizer, where the main idea is written at the top and the key details are written in the blocks beneath.

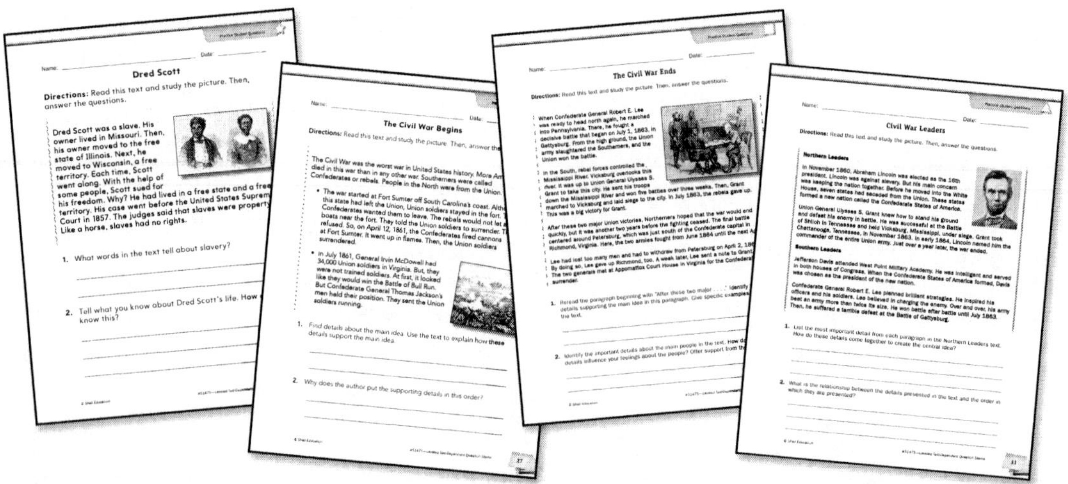

Implementing the Question Stems

This section includes 10 leveled, text-dependent question stems about identifying key details. You can implement these question stems by connecting them to the fiction passages and/or nonfiction texts that you are reading in class.

It may seem as though using question stems would be easy, but it can be a complex task for teachers. To help you see how to implement these question stems in your classroom, this section includes student pages containing texts with sample text-dependent questions. Each of the four student pages illustrates a different complexity level.

Snapshot of Differentiating a Question

The chart below models how a single leveled question stem can be tied to both literature passages and informational texts at four complexity levels. This snapshot also gives you a quick view of how the question stems differ based on the complexity levels. However, you can also see how the question stems link to one another.

	Question Stem	Literature Example	Informational Text Example
☆	How does ______ relate to ______? Give an example.	How does ice cream relate to Junie B. Jones's behavior in the grocery store? Give an example.	How do sharks relate to dolphins? Give an example.
○	How do the key details about ______ relate to the key details about ______? Include specific examples from the text.	How do the key details about the boxcar relate to the key details about the children? Include specific examples from the text.	How do the key details about electricity relate to the key details about magnetism? Include specific examples from the text.
□	Identify the key details in paragraphs ______ and ______. How do these details relate to each other? Use the text to support your answer.	Identify the key details in paragraphs 13 and 15 of chapter 7 of *Hatchet*. How do these details relate to each other? Use the text to support your answer.	Identify the key details in paragraphs 5 and 6 of the article. How do these details relate to each other? Use the text to support your answer.
△	What is the relationship between the key details in the ______ paragraph and the ______ paragraph? Use textual evidence in your response.	What is the relationship between the key details in the third paragraph and the seventh paragraph of chapter 2 in *Macbeth*? Use textual evidence in your response.	What is the relationship between the key details in the first paragraph and the fourth paragraph in the text? Use textual evidence in your response.

COMPLEXITY

LOW    

Identifying Key Details Question Stems

Use these question stems to develop your own questions for students.

- What are the details of the plot?
- Tell what you know about ______ (*character*)? How do you know this?
- What words in the text tell about the setting?
- What words in the text tell about ______ (*the main idea*)?
- How does ______ relate to ______? Give an example.
- What are the important details? How do you know?
- Why does the author tell us about ______? How do you know?
- Reread the part that starts with ". . . ." How does this part support the main idea?
- Why are the supporting details in this order?
- What is the main idea? What words from the text tell more about it?

Name: ______________________ Date: ____________

Dred Scott

Directions: Read this text and study the picture. Then, answer the questions.

Dred Scott was a slave. His owner lived in Missouri. Then, his owner moved to the free state of Illinois. Next, he moved to Wisconsin, a free territory. Each time, Scott went along. With the help of some people, Scott sued for his freedom. Why? He had lived in a free state and a free territory. His case went before the United States Supreme Court in 1857. The judges said that slaves were property! Like a horse, slaves had no rights.

1. What words in the text tell about slavery?

____

____

2. Tell what you know about Dred Scott's life. How do you know this?

____

____

____

COMPLEXITY

LOW    

Identifying Key Details Question Stems

Use these question stems to develop your own questions for students.

Use details from the text to describe the key details of the plot.

Tell the details you know about ______ (*character*) and ______ (*character*). How do these details help you to picture the characters? Use the text in your answer.

Use details from the text to tell about the setting. How do these details help you to picture it?

Find details about the main idea. Use the text to explain how these details support the main idea.

How do the key details about ______ relate to the key details about ______? Include specific examples from the text.

What are the necessary details in the paragraph/page that starts with ". . ."? How are they important to the central idea?

Why does the author include the details in the ______ paragraph/page? Use the text to prove your answer.

Reread the paragraph/page that starts with ". . . ." What details does it have to support the main idea? Use the text to explain.

Why does the author put the supporting details in this order?

What is the main idea and what information in the text tells more about it? Use examples from the text.

Name: ______________________________ Date: ______________

The Civil War Begins

Directions: Read this text and study the picture. Then, answer the questions.

The Civil War was the worst war in United States history. More Americans died in this war than in any other war. Southerners were called Confederates or rebels. People in the North were from the Union.

- The war started at Fort Sumter off South Carolina's coast. Although this state had left the Union, Union soldiers stayed in the fort. The Confederates wanted them to leave. The rebels would not let any boats near the fort. They told the Union soldiers to surrender. They refused. So, on April 12, 1861, the Confederates fired cannons at Fort Sumter. It went up in flames. Then, the Union soldiers surrendered.
- In July 1861, General Irvin McDowell had 34,000 Union soldiers in Virginia. But, they were not trained soldiers. At first, it looked like they would win the Battle of Bull Run. But Confederate General Thomas Jackson's men held their position. They sent the Union soldiers running.

1. Find details about the main idea. Use the text to explain how these details support the main idea.

____

____

2. Why does the author put the supporting details in this order?

____

____

COMPLEXITY

LOW

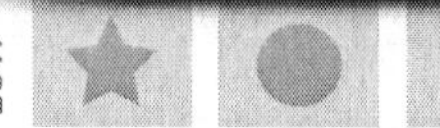

Identifying Key Details Question Stems

Use these question stems to develop your own questions for students.

Use the text to describe key details in the important events. How do these details clarify the plot?

Identify the important details about the main characters in the text. How do these details influence your feelings about the characters? Offer support from the text.

Use details from the text to describe the setting. Why does the author use these details to help you envision where the text takes place?

Identify some details about the main idea. Use text evidence to explain how these details support the main idea.

Identify the key details in paragraphs ______ and ______. How do these details relate to each other? Use the text to support your answer.

In the paragraph/page beginning with ". . ." what details are essential? How are they required to form the central idea?

What is the purpose of the details in the ______ paragraph/page? Use examples from the text to justify your response.

Reread the paragraph/page beginning with ". . . ." Identify the details supporting the main idea in this paragraph/page. Give specific examples from the text.

Why are the supporting details given in this order? How would it change the text if their order were different?

What is the main idea of the ______ paragraph/page? What key details from the text support this idea? Provide textual evidence.

Name: ______________________________ Date: ______________

The Civil War Ends

Directions: Read this text and study the picture. Then, answer the questions.

When Confederate General Robert E. Lee was ready to head north again, he marched into Pennsylvania. There, he fought a decisive battle that began on July 1, 1863, in Gettysburg. From the high ground, the Union army slaughtered the Southerners, and the Union won the battle.

In the South, rebel forces controlled the Mississippi River. Vicksburg overlooks this river. It was up to Union General Ulysses S. Grant to take this city. He sent his troops down the Mississippi River and won five battles over three weeks. Then, Grant marched to Vicksburg and laid siege to the city. In July 1863, the rebels gave up. This was a big victory for Grant.

After these two major Union victories, Northerners hoped that the war would end quickly, but it was another two years before the fighting ceased. The final battle centered around Petersburg, which was just south of the Confederate capital in Richmond, Virginia. Here, the two armies fought from June 1864 until the next April.

Lee had lost too many men and had to withdraw from Petersburg on April 2, 1865. By doing so, Lee gave up Richmond, too. A week later, Lee sent a note to Grant. The two generals met at Appomattox Court House in Virginia for the Confederate surrender.

1. Reread the paragraph beginning with "After these two major . . . ." Identify the details supporting the main idea in this paragraph. Give specific examples from the text.

____

____

2. Identify the important details about the main people in the text. How do these details influence your feelings about the people? Offer support from the text.

____

____

COMPLEXITY

LOW

Identifying Key Details Question Stems

Use these question stems to develop your own questions for students.

Explain the key details that are essential to the plot. Use textual evidence to describe why they are necessary.

Describe important details about the main characters in the text. How do these details affect your overall understanding of the characters? Provide textual evidence.

What details does the author use to describe the setting, and how do these details enhance your understanding of the text?

Identify some details about the main idea. Describe how the details support the main idea. Justify your answer using evidence from the text.

What is the relationship between the key details in the ______ paragraph and the ______ paragraph? Use textual evidence in your response.

List the most important detail from each paragraph/page in the text. How do these details come together to create the central idea?

What is the purpose of the details in the ______ paragraph/page? Provide textual evidence.

Reread the paragraph/page beginning with ". . ." to identify the details it contains that support the main idea. Provide specific examples from the text in your response.

What is the relationship between the details presented in the text and the order in which they are presented?

What is the main idea of the ______ paragraph/page? Identify the key details supporting this idea. Provide textual evidence.

Name: ______________________________ Date: ______________

Civil War Leaders

Directions: Read this text and study the picture. Then, answer the questions.

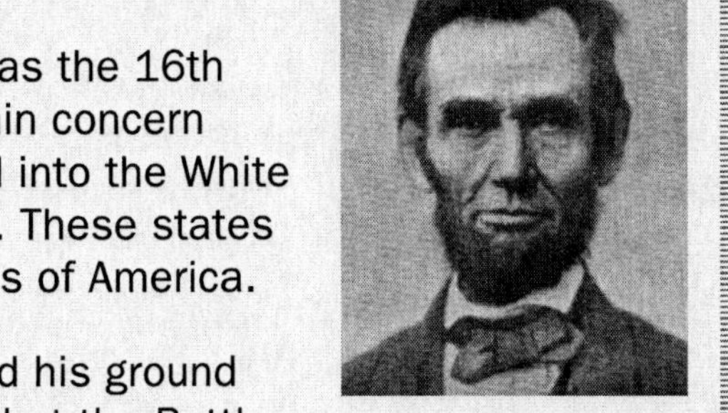

Northern Leaders

In November 1860, Abraham Lincoln was elected as the 16th president. Lincoln was against slavery. But his main concern was keeping the nation together. Before he moved into the White House, seven states had seceded from the Union. These states formed a new nation called the Confederate States of America.

Union General Ulysses S. Grant knew how to stand his ground and defeat his enemy in battle. He was successful at the Battle of Shiloh in Tennessee and held Vicksburg, Mississippi, under siege. Grant took Chattanooga, Tennessee, in November 1863. In early 1864, Lincoln named him the commander of the entire Union army. Just over a year later, the war ended.

Southern Leaders

Jefferson Davis attended West Point Military Academy. He was intelligent and served in both houses of Congress. When the Confederate States of America formed, Davis was chosen as the president of the new nation.

Confederate General Robert E. Lee planned brilliant strategies. He inspired his officers and his soldiers. Lee believed in charging the enemy. Over and over, his army beat an army more than twice its size. He won battle after battle until July 1863. Then, he suffered a terrible defeat at the Battle of Gettysburg.

1. List the most important detail from each paragraph in the Northern Leaders text. How do these details come together to create the central idea?

____

____

____

2. What is the relationship between the details presented in the text and the order in which they are presented?

____

____

____

Identifying Key Details K–12 Alignment

Use this chart to determine the best question stems for your different groups of students.

☆	○	□	△
What are the details of the plot?	Use details from the text to describe the key details of the plot.	Use the text to describe key details in the important events. How do these details clarify the plot?	Explain the key details that are essential to the plot. Use textual evidence to describe why they are necessary.
Tell what you know about ______ (*character*). How do you know this?	Tell the details you know about ______ (*character*) and ______ (*character*). How do these details help you to picture the characters? Use the text in your answer.	Identify the important details about the main characters in the text. How do these details influence your feelings about the characters? Offer support from the text.	Describe important details about the main characters in the text. How do these details affect your overall understanding of the characters? Provide textual evidence.
What words in the text tell about the setting?	Use details from the text to tell about the setting. How do these details help you to picture it?	Use details from the text to describe the setting. Why does the author use these details to help you envision where the text takes place?	What details does the author use to describe the setting, and how do these details enhance your understanding of the text?
What words in the text tell about ______ (*the main idea*)?	Find details about the main idea. Use the text to explain how these details support the main idea.	Identify some details about the main idea. Use text evidence to explain how these details support the main idea.	Identify some details about the main idea. Describe how the details support the main idea. Justify your answer using evidence from the text.
How does ______ relate to ______? Give an example.	How do the key details about ______ relate to the key details about ______? Include specific examples from the text.	Identify the key details in paragraphs ______ and ______. How do these details relate to each other? Use the text to support your answer.	What is the relationship between the key details in the ______ paragraph and the ______ paragraph? Use textual evidence in your response.

Identifying Key Details K–12 Alignment *(cont.)*

★	●	■	▲
What are the important details? How do you know?	What are the necessary details in the paragraph/page that starts with ". . ."? How are they important to the central idea?	In the paragraph/page beginning with ". . ." what details are essential? How are they required to form the central idea?	List the most important detail from each paragraph/page in the text. How do these details come together to create the central idea?
Why does the author tell us about ______? How do you know?	Why does the author include the details in the ______ paragraph/page? Use the text to prove your answer.	What is the purpose of the details in the ______ paragraph/page? Use examples from the text to justify your response.	What is the purpose of the details in the ______ paragraph/page? Provide textual evidence.
Reread the part that starts with ". . . ." How does this part support the main idea?	Reread the paragraph/page that starts with ". . . ." What details does it have to support the main idea? Use the text to explain.	Reread the paragraph/page beginning with ". . . ." Identify the details supporting the main idea in this paragraph/page. Give specific examples from the text.	Reread the paragraph/page beginning with ". . ." to identify the details it contains that support the main idea. Provide specific examples from the text in your response.
Why are the supporting details in this order?	Why does the author put the supporting details in this order?	Why are the supporting details given in this order? How would it change the text if their order were different?	What is the relationship between the details presented in the text and the order in which they are presented?
What is the main idea? What words from the text tell more about it?	What is the main idea, and what information in the text tells more about it? Use examples from the text.	What is the main idea of the ______ paragraph/page? What key details from the text support this idea? Provide textual evidence.	What is the main idea of the ______ paragraph/page? Identify the key details supporting this idea. Provide textual evidence.

Summarizing

Skill Overview

Summarizing is the marriage of main idea or theme and the key details that support it. When students put information into their own words, it increases both their immediate understanding and long-term retention of material. Summarizing means pulling out only the essential elements of a text or passage. Therefore, it is best to teach after you have already used some of the questions from the following sections: *Understanding Main Idea and Theme* and *Identifying Key Details*.

A student's ability to "sum up" what's been read is critical to comprehension. Ask students to retell the text, making sure that the events are shared in the sequence that they occur. You can use graphic organizers with numbers or arrows in your think-alouds with the class.

Teach these basic steps of summarizing:

- Look for a main idea/theme sentence; if there is none, create one.
- Find the key details (phrases or sentences) that support the main idea/theme.
- Group all related terms or ideas.
- Put the summary together.

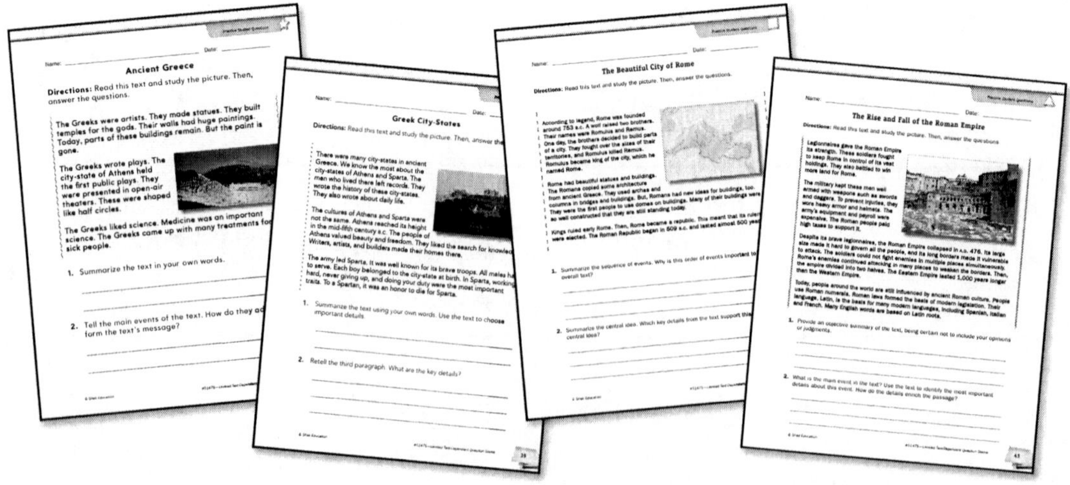

Implementing the Question Stems

This section includes 10 leveled, text-dependent question stems about summarizing. You can implement these question stems by connecting them to the fiction passages and/or nonfiction texts that you are reading in class.

It may seem as though using question stems would be easy, but it can be a complex task for teachers. To help you see how to implement these question stems in your classroom, this section includes student pages containing texts with sample text-dependent questions. Each of the four student pages illustrates a different complexity level.

Snapshot of Differentiating a Question

The chart below models how a single leveled question stem can be tied to both literature passages and informational texts at four complexity levels. This snapshot also gives you a quick view of how the question stems differ based on the complexity levels. However, you can also see how the question stems are linked to one another.

	Question Stem	Literature Example	Informational Text Example
☆	What happens in the text?	What happens in *Chicka Chicka Boom Boom*?	What happens in the story about Abraham Lincoln's childhood?
○	What is the main event in the text? Tell the most important details about this event.	What is the main event in *Cam Jansen and the End of The World*? Tell the most important details about this event.	What is the main event in this chapter of *The Liberty Bell*? Tell the most important details about this event.
□	What is the main event in the text? Use the text to identify the most important details about this event.	What is the main event in this chapter of *Tuck Everlasting*? Use the text to identify the most important details about this event.	What is the main event in this chapter about the Roman Empire? Use the text to identify the most important details about this event.
△	What is the text's main event? Use the text to identify the most important details about this event. How do these details enrich the text?	What is the main event in *The Scarlett Letter*? Use the text to identify the most important details about this event. How do these details enrich the novel?	What were the main events in the life of Maya Angelou? Use the text to identify the most important details about these events. How do the details enrich the biography?

COMPLEXITY

LOW    

Summarizing Question Stems

Use these question stems to develop your own questions for students.

Retell the main events of the text in order.

Summarize the text in your own words.

What happens in the text?

Retell the text's events in order. Why does the order of events matter?

Retell the text in your own words. Give details from the text.

Retell the ______ paragraph/page. Give details from the text.

Retell the text. Start with the main idea. Add the important details.

Tell the text's events in the order they happened.

Tell the main events of the text. How do they add up to form the text's message?

Retell only the text's events.

Name: ______________________________ Date: ______________

Ancient Greece

Directions: Read this text and study the picture. Then, answer the questions.

The Greeks were artists. They made statues. They built temples for the gods. Their walls had huge paintings. Today, parts of these buildings remain. But the paint is gone.

The Greeks wrote plays. The city-state of Athens held the first public plays. They were presented in open-air theaters. These were shaped like half circles.

The Greeks liked science. Medicine was an important science. The Greeks came up with many treatments for sick people.

1. Summarize the text in your own words.

____

____

2. Tell the main events of the text. How do they add up to form the text's message?

____

____

Summarizing Question Stems

Use these question stems to develop your own questions for students.

Retell the text by listing the key details from the text in the order in which they happen.

Summarize the text using your own words. Use the text to choose important details.

What is the main event in the text? Tell the most important details about this event.

Retell what happens in order. How is the order of events important to the text?

Retell the text in your own words. Use the text to add details.

Retell the ______ paragraph/page. What are the key details?

Retell the text, starting with the main idea. Be sure to add important details.

Tell the text's events in the order in which they occur. Do not add your opinions.

Tell the text's main events. How do they help to create the text's message?

Give a text summary. Do not add your opinions or judgments.

Name: ____________________ Date: __________

Greek City-States

Directions: Read this text and study the picture. Then, answer the questions.

There were many city-states in ancient Greece. We know the most about the city-states of Athens and Sparta. The men who lived there left records. They wrote the history of these city-states. They also wrote about daily life.

The cultures of Athens and Sparta were not the same. Athens reached its height in the mid-fifth century B.C. The people of Athens valued beauty and freedom. They liked the search for knowledge. Writers, artists, and builders made their homes there.

The army led Sparta. It was well known for its brave troops. All males had to serve. Each boy belonged to the city-state at birth. In Sparta, working hard, never giving up, and doing your duty were the most important traits. To a Spartan, it was an honor to die for Sparta.

1. Summarize the text using your own words. Use the text to choose important details.

____

____

2. Retell the third paragraph. What are the key details?

____

____

____

COMPLEXITY

LOW    

Summarizing Question Stems

Use these question stems to develop your own questions for students.

Summarize the text by recounting specific key details from the text in the order in which they occur.

Summarize the text in your own words. Refer back to the text to explain the details you include.

What is the main event in the text? Use the text to identify the most important details about this event.

Summarize the sequence of events. Why is this order of events important to the overall text?

Retell the text in your own words, adding specific details from the text.

Summarize the ______ paragraph/page. Include key details from the text.

Summarize the central idea. Which key details from the text support this central idea?

Summarize what occurs in the text without including your personal opinions.

Summarize the main events of the text. How do these events relate to the overall message of the text?

Create a summary of the text. Do not include your opinions or judgments.

Name: ______________________________ Date: ______________

The Beautiful City of Rome

Directions: Read this text and study the picture. Then, answer the questions.

According to legend, Rome was founded around 753 B.C. A wolf raised two brothers. Their names were Romulus and Remus. One day, the brothers decided to build parts of a city. They fought over the sizes of their territories, and Romulus killed Remus. Romulus became king of the city, which he named Rome.

Rome had beautiful statues and buildings. The Romans copied some architecture from ancient Greece. They used arches and columns in bridges and buildings. But, Romans had new ideas for buildings, too. They were the first people to use domes on buildings. Many of their buildings were so well constructed that they are still standing today.

Kings ruled early Rome. Then, Rome became a republic. This meant that its rulers were elected. The Roman Republic began in 509 B.C. and lasted almost 500 years.

1. Summarize the sequence of events. Why is this order of events important to the overall text?

____

____

____

2. Summarize the central idea. Which key details from the text support this central idea?

____

____

____

Summarizing Question Stems

Use these question stems to develop your own questions for students.

Summarize the text by recounting specific key details from the text in sequence.

Summarize the text in your own words, referencing the text to validate the details you include.

What is the main event in the text? Use the text to identify the most important details about this event. How do the details enrich the text?

What is the sequence of events in the text? How does this sequence add to the overall effect of the text?

Retell the text in your own words, including specific textual details.

Summarize the ______ paragraph/page, including key details from the text.

Summarize the central idea and identify the specific details from the text that support this idea.

Summarize the sequence of events in the text without revealing your personal opinions or judgments about the text.

Summarize the main events of the text, and explain how these events relate to the text's underlying message.

Provide an objective summary of the text, being certain not to include your opinions or judgments.

Name: ______________________________ Date: ______________

The Rise and Fall of the Roman Empire

Directions: Read this text and study the picture. Then, answer the questions.

Legionnaires gave the Roman Empire its strength. These soldiers fought to keep Rome in control of its vast holdings. They also battled to win more land for Rome.

The military kept these men well armed with weapons such as swords and daggers. To prevent injuries, they wore heavy armor and helmets. The army's equipment and payroll were expensive. The Roman people paid high taxes to support it.

Despite its brave legionnaires, the Roman Empire collapsed in A.D. 476. Its large size made it hard to govern all the people, and its long borders made it vulnerable to attack. The soldiers could not fight enemies in multiple places simultaneously. Rome's enemies continued attacking in many places to weaken the borders. Then, the empire divided into two halves. The Eastern Empire lasted 1,000 years longer than the Western Empire.

Today, people around the world are still influenced by ancient Roman culture. People use Roman numerals. Roman laws formed the basis of modern legislation. Their language, Latin, is the basis for many modern languages, including Spanish, Italian and French. Many English words are based on Latin roots.

1. Provide an objective summary of the text, being certain not to include your opinions or judgments.

____

____

____

2. What is the main event in the text? Use the text to identify the most important details about this event. How do the details enrich the passage?

____

____

____

Summarizing K–12 Alignment

Use this chart to determine the best question stems for your different groups of students.

☆	○	□	△
Retell the main events of the text in order.	Retell the text by listing the key details from the text in the order in which they happened.	Summarize the text by recounting specific key details from the text in the order in which they occur.	Summarize the text by recounting specific key details from the text in sequence.
Summarize the text in your own words.	Summarize the text using your own words. Use the text to choose important details.	Summarize the text in your own words. Refer back to the text to explain the details you include.	Summarize the text in your own words, referencing the text to validate the details you include.
What happens in the text?	What is the main event in the text? Tell the most important details about this event.	What is the main event in the text? Use the text to identify the most important details about this event.	What is the main event in the text? Use the text to identify the most important details about this event. How do the details enrich the text?
Retell the text's events in order. Why does the order of events matter?	Retell what happens in order. How is the order of events important to the text?	Summarize the sequence of events. Why is this order of events important to the overall text?	What is the sequence of events in the text? How does this sequence add to the overall effect of the text?
Retell the text in your own words. Give details from the text.	Retell the text in your own words. Use the text to add details.	Retell the text in your own words, adding specific details from the text.	Retell the text in your own words, including specific textual details.

Summarizing K–12 Alignment *(cont.)*

☆	○	□	△
Retell the ______ paragraph/page. Give details from the text.	Retell the ______ paragraph/page. What are the key details?	Summarize the ______ paragraph/page. Include key details from the text.	Summarize the ______ paragraph/page, including key details from the text.
Retell the text. Start with the main idea. Add the important details.	Retell the text, starting with the main idea. Be sure to add important details.	Summarize the central idea. Which key details from the text support this central idea?	Summarize the central idea and identify the specific details from the text that support this idea.
Tell the text's events in the order they happened.	Tell the text's events in the order in which they occur. Do not add your opinions.	Summarize what occurs in the text without including your personal opinions.	Summarize the sequence of events in the text without revealing your personal opinions or judgments about the text.
Tell the main events of the text. How do they add up to form the text's message?	Tell the text's main events. How do they help to create the text's message?	Summarize the main events of the text. How do these events relate to the overall message of the text?	Summarize the main events of the text, and explain how these events relate to the text's underlying message.
Retell only the text's events.	Give a text summary. Do not add your opinions or judgments.	Create a summary of the text. Do not include your opinions or judgments.	Provide an objective summary of the text, being certain not to include your opinions or judgments.

Using Text Features

Skill Overview

Far too often students ignore the information they can gather from text features, especially in informational text. In literature, print shown in boldface, italics, or solid caps is done to provide emphasis. That's why it's a good idea to use text-dependent questions to make your students look for, and use, text features. Illustrations, sidebars, graphs, and charts are used in both informational text and literature to make a point, support facts in the running text, and improve comprehension.

Prior to teaching a text, glance through it and note all of its text features. You know to look from an asterisk at the end of a word to the bottom of the page for additional information, but your students may not. Be ready with a text-dependent question that will draw students' attention to each text feature. If this is done with each text, over time students' ability to independently read text with greater comprehension will be sharpened.

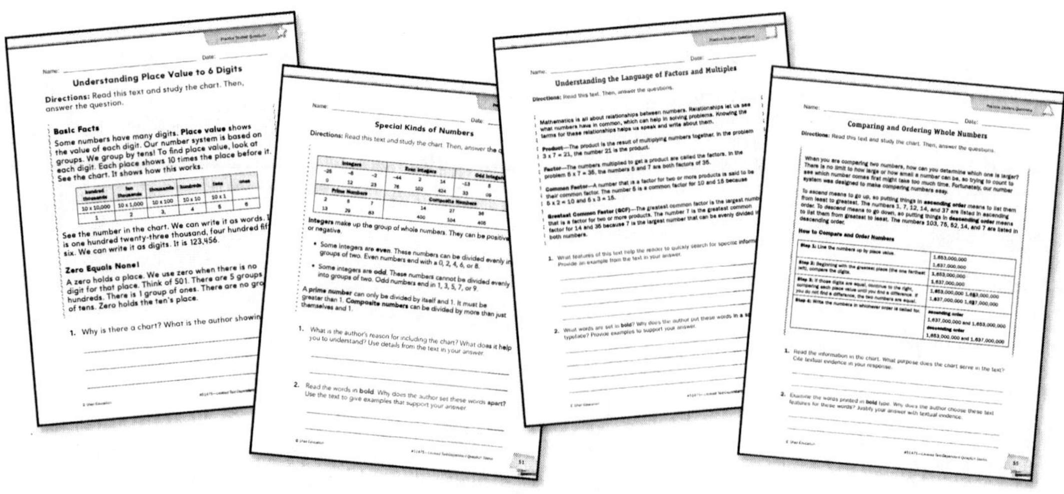
Understanding Place Value to 6 Digits
Special Kinds of Numbers
Understanding the Language of Factors and Multiples
Comparing and Ordering Whole Numbers

Implementing the Question Stems

This section includes 10 leveled, text-dependent question stems about using text features. You can implement these question stems by connecting them to the fiction passages and/or nonfiction texts that you are reading in class.

It may seem as though using question stems would be easy, but it can be a complex task for teachers. To help you see how to implement these question stems in your classroom, this section includes student pages containing texts with sample text-dependent questions. Each of the four student pages illustrates a different complexity level.

Snapshot of Differentiating a Question

The chart below models how a single leveled question stem can be tied to both literature passages and informational texts at four complexity levels. This snapshot also gives you a quick view of how the question stems differ based on the complexity levels. However, you can also see how the question stems link to one another.

	Question Stem	Literature Example	Informational Text Example
☆	Why does the author include ______ (*text feature*)? What does it tell you?	Why does the author include the dates in the journal? What do they tell you?	Why does the author include the boldface text? What does it tell you?
○	What is the purpose of the ______ (*text feature*) on page ______? What do you learn from it?	What is the purpose of the word in all capital letters on page 24? What did you learn from it?	What is the purpose of the side heading on page 56? What did you learn from them?
□	Why does the author include the (*text feature*) on page ______? What specific information does it give the reader? Why is this important?	Why does the author include the sidebar on page 118? What specific information does it give the reader? Why is this important?	Why does the author include the graphics on page 281? What specific information do they give the reader? Why is this important?
△	What is the author's purpose in including the ______ (*text feature*) on page ______? What is the importance of the information it conveys to the reader?	What is the author's purpose in including the sketch on page 67? What is the importance of the information it conveys to the reader?	What is the author's purpose in including the footnote on page 319? What is the importance of the information it conveys to the reader?

Using Text Features Question Stems

Use these question stems to develop your own questions for students.

Look at the sidebar/graphic. Why is it there? What does it tell you?

Look at the headings. How do they guide the reader? Explain.

Why does the author include ______ (*text feature*)? What does it tell you?

Look at the table of contents/index. What kind of information does it show you?

Why is there ______ (*text feature*)? What is the author showing you?

What information do you expect to find under the heading ______? Why?

Look at the words in *italics* and **bold**. Why does the author make these words different?

What is shown on the front of the book? The back of the book? Why are those things there?

Which parts of the text help you to look for information? How?

Read the headings. How are they alike? How are they different?

Name: ______________________ Date: __________

Understanding Place Value to 6 Digits

Directions: Read this text and study the chart. Then, answer the question.

Basic Facts

Some numbers have many digits. **Place value** shows the value of each digit. Our number system is based on groups. We group by tens! To find place value, look at each digit. Each place shows 10 times the place before it. See the chart. It shows how this works.

hundred thousands	ten thousands	thousands	hundreds	tens	ones
10 x 10,000	10 x 1,000	10 x 100	10 x 10	10 x 1	
1	2	3	4	5	6

See the number in the chart. We can write it as words. It is one hundred twenty-three thousand, four hundred fifty-six. We can write it as digits. It is 123,456.

Zero Equals None!

A zero holds a place. We use zero when there is no digit for that place. Think of 501. There are 5 groups of hundreds. There is 1 group of ones. There are no groups of tens. Zero holds the ten's place.

1. Why is there a chart? What is the author showing you?

____

____

____

COMPLEXITY

LOW    

Using Text Features Question Stems

Use these question stems to develop your own questions for students.

Read the sidebars/graphics. Why does the author include these? What can you learn from them? Give examples.

Read the headings. How do they help you move through the text? Give specific examples.

What is the purpose of the _____ (*text feature*) on page _____? What do you learn from it?

Look at the table of contents/index. What kind of information does it show you? How can you use the table of contents/index to find _____ in the book?

What is the author's reason for including the _____ (*text feature*)? What does it help you to understand? Use details from the text in your answer.

How does the subheading on page _____ relate to the heading on page _____? How does this help the reader?

Read the words in *italics* and **bold**. Why does the author set these words apart with a different type? Use the text to give examples that support your answer.

What information is given on the front cover? The back cover? Why is this information on the outside of the book?

What features help you to look for information? Give an example.

Tell how the headings are alike and different. Use examples from the text.

Name: ______________________________ Date: ______________

Special Kinds of Numbers

Directions: Read this text and study the chart. Then, answer the questions.

Integers			Even Integers			Odd Integers		
–25	–5	–2	–44	2	14	–13	5	17
0	12	23	76	102	424	33	09	441
Prime Numbers			**Composite Numbers**					
2	5	7	14	27	36			
13	29	83	400	104	405			

Integers make up the group of whole numbers. They can be positive or negative.

- Some integers are **even**. These numbers can be divided evenly into groups of two. Even numbers end with a 0, 2, 4, 6, or 8.
- Some integers are **odd**. These numbers cannot be divided evenly into groups of two. Odd numbers end in 1, 3, 5, 7, or 9.

A **prime number** can only be divided by itself and 1. It must be greater than 1. **Composite numbers** can be divided by more than just themselves and 1.

1. What is the author's reason for including the chart? What does it help you to understand? Use details from the text in your answer.

____

____

2. Read the words in **bold**. Why does the author set these words apart? Use the text to give examples that support your answer.

____

____

COMPLEXITY

LOW    

Using Text Features Question Stems

Use these question stems to develop your own questions for students.

Read the information in the sidebars/graphics. What purpose do they serve in the text? Provide text evidence in your answer.

Review the headings in the text or chapter. How do the headings create the structure for the text? Cite specific examples.

Why does the author include the ______ (*text feature*) on page ______? What specific information does it give the reader? Why is this important?

Explain how you could use this table of contents/index to do research about ______. Provide specific information from the text.

What is the purpose of the ______ (*text feature*)? What does the author want to emphasize? Refer to the text in your response.

Why is there a heading on page ______ and a subheading on page ______? What does this format do for the reader?

What words are set in *italics* and **bold**? Why does the author put these words in a special typeface? Provide examples to support your answer.

What appears on the front cover? What appears on the back cover? Why is this information included on the outside of the book?

What features of this text help the reader to quickly search for specific information? Provide an example from the text in your answer.

Scan the headings. What kind of information will you find in this text? Provide specific examples.

Name: ______________________ Date: ____________

Understanding the Language of Factors and Multiples

Directions: Read this text. Then, answer the questions.

Mathematics is all about relationships between numbers. Relationships let us see what numbers have in common, which can help in solving problems. Knowing the terms for these relationships helps us speak and write about them.

Product—The product is the result of multiplying numbers together. In the problem 3 x 7 = 21, the number 21 is the product.

Factor—The numbers multiplied to get a product are called the factors. In the problem 5 x 7 = 35, the numbers 5 and 7 are both factors of 35.

Common Factor—A number that is a factor for two or more products is said to be their common factor. The number 5 is a common factor for 10 and 15 because 5 x 2 = 10 and 5 x 3 = 15.

Greatest Common Factor (GCF)—The greatest common factor is the largest number that is a factor for two or more products. The number 7 is the greatest common factor for 14 and 35 because 7 is the largest number that can be evenly divided into both numbers.

1. What features of this text help the reader to quickly search for specific information? Provide an example from the text in your answer.

____

____

____

____

2. What words are set in **bold**? Why does the author put these words in a special typeface? Provide examples to support your answer.

____

____

____

____

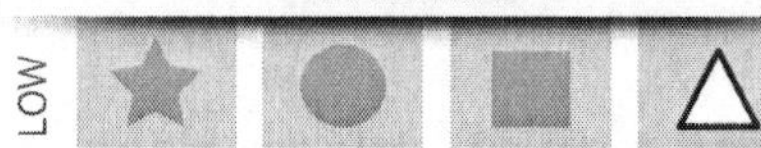

Using Text Features Question Stems

Use these question stems to develop your own questions for students.

Read the information in the sidebars/graphics. What purpose do these sidebars/graphics serve in the text? Cite textual evidence in your response.

Review the headings in the text or chapter. How do these headings relate to the structure of the text? Cite specific examples from the text in your answer.

What is the author's purpose in including the ______ (*text feature*) on page ______? What is the importance of the information it conveys to the reader?

Provide a specific example of how a reader would use the table of contents/index to get information. How could you use the table of contents/index in this book to do research on ______?

Describe the author's purpose in choosing to include ______ (*text feature*) in the text. Refer to the text in your explanation.

What is the relationship between the heading on page ______ and the subheading on page ______? How does this text feature help the reader?

Examine the words printed in *italics* and **bold** type. Why does the author choose these text features for these words? Justify your answer with textual evidence.

What information is presented on the front and back covers of the book? Why is this information chosen to be on the book's exterior?

What particular features of this text help the reader to scan for specific information? Cite an example from the text to illustrate your response.

What can you conclude from scanning the headings? Justify your response with specific examples from the text.

Name: ______________________________ Date: ______________

Comparing and Ordering Whole Numbers

Directions: Read this text and study the chart. Then, answer the questions.

When you are comparing two numbers, how can you determine which one is larger? There is no limit to how large or how small a number can be, so trying to count to see which number comes first might take too much time. Fortunately, our number system was designed to make comparing numbers easy.

To *ascend* means to go up, so putting things in **ascending order** means to list them from least to greatest. The numbers 1, 7, 12, 14, and 37 are listed in ascending order. To *descend* means to go down, so putting things in **descending order** means to list them from greatest to least. The numbers 103, 75, 52, 14, and 7 are listed in descending order.

How to Compare and Order Numbers

Step 1: Line the numbers up by place value.	1,653,000,000 1,637,000,000
Step 2: Beginning with the greatest place (the one farthest left), compare the digits.	**1**,653,000,000 **1**,637,000,000
Step 3: If those digits are equal, continue to the right, comparing each place value until you find a difference. If you do not find a difference, the two numbers are equal.	1,**6**53,000,000 1,6**5**3,000,000 1,**6**37,000,000 1,6**3**7,000,000
Step 4: Write the numbers in whichever order is called for.	**ascending order** 1,637,000,000 and 1,653,000,000 **descending order** 1,653,000,000 and 1,637,000,000

1. Read the information in the chart. What purpose does the chart serve in the text? Cite textual evidence in your response.

____

____

2. Examine the words printed in **bold** type. Why does the author choose these text features for these words? Justify your answer with textual evidence.

____

____

Using Text Features K–12 Alignment

Use this chart to determine the best question stems for your different groups of students.

☆	○	□	△
Look at the sidebar/ graphic. Why is it there? What does it tell you?	Read the sidebars/ graphics. Why does the author include these? What can you learn from them? Give examples.	Read the information in the sidebars/ graphics. What purpose do they serve in the text? Provide text evidence in your answer.	Read the information in the sidebars/graphics. What purpose do these sidebars/graphics serve in the text? Cite textual evidence in your response.
Look at the headings. How do they guide the reader? Explain.	Read the headings. How do they help you move through the text? Give specific examples.	Review the headings in the text or chapter. How do the headings create the structure for the text? Cite specific examples.	Review the headings in the text or chapter. How do these headings relate to the structure of the text? Cite specific examples from the text in your answer.
Why does the author include ______ (*text feature*)? What does it tell you?	What is the purpose of the ______ (*text feature*) on page ______? What do you learn from it?	Why does the author include the ______ (*text feature*) on page ______? What specific information does it give the reader? Why is this important?	What is the author's purpose in including the ______ (*text feature*) on page ______? What is the importance of the information it conveys to the reader?
Look at the table of contents/index. What kind of information does it show you?	Look at the table of contents/index. What kind of information does it show you? How can you use the table of contents/ index to find ______ in the book?	Explain how you can use this table of contents/index to do research about ______. Provide specific information from the text.	Provide a specific example of how a reader would use the table of contents/index to get information. How could you use the table of contents/index in this book to do research on ______?
Why is there ______ (*text feature*)? What is the author showing you?	What is the author's reason for including the ______ (*text feature*)? What does it help you to understand? Use details from the text in your answer.	What is the purpose of the ______ (*text feature*)? What does the author want to emphasize? Refer to the text in your response.	Describe the author's purpose in choosing to include ______ (*text feature*) in the text. Refer to the text in your explanation.

Using Text Features K–12 Alignment *(cont.)*

★	●	■	▲
What information do you expect to find under the heading ______? Why?	How does the subheading on page ______ relate to the heading on page ______? How does this help the reader?	Why is there a heading on page ______ and a subheading on page ______? What does this format do for the reader?	What is the relationship between the heading on page ______ and the subheading on page ______? How does this text feature help the reader?
Look at the words in *italics* and **bold**. Why does the author make these words different?	Read the words in *italics* and **bold**. Why does the author set these words apart with a different type? Use the text to give examples that support your answer.	What words are set in *italics* and **bold**? Why does the author put these words in a special typeface? Provide examples to support your answer.	Examine the words printed in *italics* and **bold** type. Why does the author choose these text features for these words? Justify your answer with textual evidence.
What is shown on the front of the book? The back of the book? Why are those things there?	What information is given on the front cover? The back cover? Why is this information on the outside of the book?	What appears on the front cover? What appears on the back cover? Why is this information included on the outside of the book?	What information is presented on the front and back covers of the book? Why is this information chosen to be on the book's exterior?
Which parts of the text help you to look for information? How?	What features help you to look for information? Give an example.	What features of this text help the reader to quickly search for specific information? Provide an example from the text in your answer.	What particular features of this text help the reader to scan for specific information? Cite an example from the text to illustrate your response.
Read the headings. How are they alike? How are they different?	Tell how the headings are alike and different. Use examples from the text.	Scan the headings. What kind of information will you find in this text? Provide specific examples.	What can you conclude from scanning the headings? Justify your response with specific examples from the text.

Identifying the Setting

Skill Overview

The setting is the time, place, and overall environment in which a piece of literature occurs. As a result, the events of the plot can happen in the past, the present, or the future—or all three. The overall environment is an important concept, especially when the text occurs in the past, the future, or in another dimension, since it may provide constraints on the characters that students have to imagine because they differ so much from present reality.

When reading nonfiction pieces, setting needs to be viewed in a different way. The "setting" in a nonfiction text still relates to when and where the text takes place. However, instead of being part of the storytelling, it gives important background information to the reader. A text on George Washington Carver would be set in a very different time and place than a text describing Marie Antoinette. A description of a groundbreaking science finding would have a very different environment than a text about how to add numbers.

Once your students understand the elements of setting, use text-dependent questions to have them analyze how the setting affects the characters, tone, mood, or other aspects of the text.

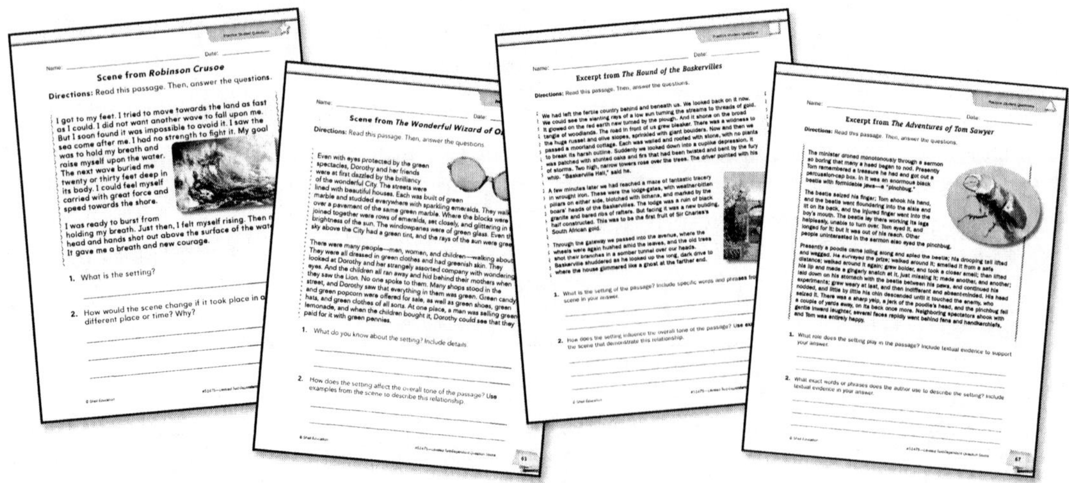

Implementing the Question Stems

This section includes 10 leveled, text-dependent question stems about identifying the setting. You can implement these question stems by connecting them to the fiction passages and/or nonfiction texts that you are reading in class.

It may seem as though using question stems would be easy, but it can be a complex task for teachers. To help you see how to implement these question stems in your classroom, this section includes student pages containing texts with sample text-dependent questions. Each of the four student pages illustrates a different complexity level.

Snapshot of Differentiating a Question

The chart below models how a single leveled question stem can be tied to both literature passages and informational texts at four complexity levels. This snapshot also gives you a quick view of how the question stems differ based on the complexity levels. However, you can also see how the question stems link to one another.

	Question Stem	Literature Example	Informational Text Example
☆	How does setting affect the life of ______(*character*)? How do you know?	How does setting affect the life of Puss in Boots? How do you know?	How does setting affect the life of Thomas Jefferson? How do you know?
○	How is ______ (*character's*) life affected by the setting? Explain.	How is Laura Ingalls's life affected by the setting? Explain.	How is Susan B. Anthony's life affected by the setting? Explain.
□	How is ______ (*character's*) life influenced by the setting? Give details in your explanation.	How is Stanley Yelnats's life influenced by the setting? Give details in your explanation.	How is Mark Antony's life influenced by the setting? Give details in your explanation.
△	What impact does the setting have on ______(*character's*) life? Include specific details in your explanation.	What impact does the setting have on Dr. Jekyll's life? Include specific details in your explanation.	What impact does the setting have on Edgar Allan Poe's life? Include specific details in your explanation.

COMPLEXITY

LOW    

Identifying the Setting Question Stems

Use these question stems to develop your own questions for students.

- What is the setting?
- How does the setting affect the text? Give an example.
- Why is the time period of the text important? How do you know?
- Tell what you know about the setting. Give details.
- How would the text change if it took place in a different place or time? Why?
- How is the setting related to ______ (*character*)? Why?
- How does setting affect the life of ______ (*character*)? How do you know?
- How does the text's setting relate to its theme? How do you know?
- How does the text's setting relate to its tone? Tell how you know.
- What does the author tell you about the setting? Give an example.

Name: ______________________ Date: ____________

Scene from *Robinson Crusoe*

Directions: Read this passage. Then, answer the questions.

I got to my feet. I tried to move towards the land as fast as I could. I did not want another wave to fall upon me. But I soon found it was impossible to avoid it. I saw the sea come after me. I had no strength to fight it. My goal was to hold my breath and raise myself upon the water. The next wave buried me twenty or thirty feet deep in its body. I could feel myself carried with great force and speed towards the shore.

I was ready to burst from holding my breath. Just then, I felt myself rising. Then my head and hands shot out above the surface of the water. It gave me a breath and new courage.

1. What is the setting?

____

2. How would the scene change if it took place in a different place or time? Why?

____

____

____

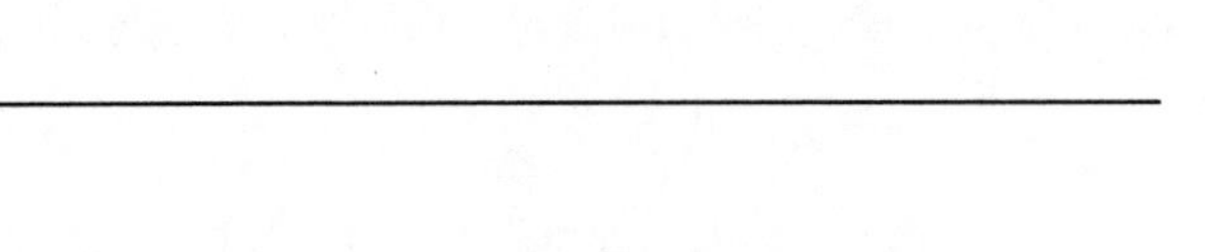

COMPLEXITY

LOW 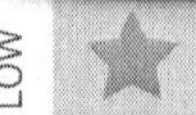   

Identifying the Setting Question Stems

Use these question stems to develop your own questions for students.

Describe the setting. Use words and phrases from the text.

How does the setting influence the text? Give an example from the text.

How does the time period influence the text? Use the text to explain.

What do you know about the setting? Include details.

How would the text change if it took place in a different place or time? Use the text to explain.

How does the setting relate to ______ (*character*)? Explain using examples from the text.

How is ______ (*character's*) life affected by the setting? Explain.

How does the setting of the text relate to its theme? Explain.

How does the setting affect the overall tone of the text? Use examples from the text to describe this relationship.

How does the author describe the setting? Give an example.

Name: ______________________________ Date: ______________

Scene from *The Wonderful Wizard of Oz*

Directions: Read this passage. Then, answer the questions.

Even with eyes protected by the green spectacles, Dorothy and her friends were at first dazzled by the brilliancy of the wonderful City. The streets were lined with beautiful houses. Each was built of green marble and studded everywhere with sparkling emeralds. They walked over a pavement of the same green marble. Where the blocks were joined together were rows of emeralds, set closely, and glittering in the brightness of the sun. The windowpanes were of green glass. Even the sky above the City had a green tint, and the rays of the sun were green.

There were many people—men, women, and children—walking about. They were all dressed in green clothes and had greenish skin. They looked at Dorothy and her strangely assorted company with wondering eyes. And the children all ran away and hid behind their mothers when they saw the Lion. No one spoke to them. Many shops stood in the street, and Dorothy saw that everything in them was green. Green candy and green popcorn were offered for sale, as well as green shoes, green hats, and green clothes of all sorts. At one place, a man was selling green lemonade, and when the children bought it, Dorothy could see that they paid for it with green pennies.

1. What do you know about the setting? Include details.

____

____

2. How does the setting affect the overall tone of the passage? Use examples from the scene to describe this relationship.

____

____

COMPLEXITY

LOW

Identifying the Setting Question Stems

Use these question stems to develop your own questions for students.

What is the setting of the text? Include specific words and phrases from the text in your answer.

What role does the setting play in the text? Include examples from the text to support your answer.

What impact does the time period have on the text? Include a text example to support your answer.

Use details from the text to describe the setting.

How would the text be different if it occurred in another time or place? Provide text evidence to support your answer.

What is the connection between the setting and character development in the text? Support your answer with examples from the text.

How is ______ (*character's*) life influenced by the setting? Give details in your explanation.

What is the connection between the setting and the theme? Support your answer with examples from the text.

How does the setting influence the overall tone of the text? Use examples from the text that demonstrate this relationship.

How is the setting described? Use the text to explain your answer.

Name: ______________________ Date: ____________

Excerpt from *The Hound of the Baskervilles*

Directions: Read this passage. Then, answer the questions.

We had left the fertile country behind and beneath us. We looked back on it now. We could see the slanting rays of a low sun turning the streams to threads of gold. It glowed on the red earth new turned by the plough. And it shone on the broad tangle of woodlands. The road in front of us grew bleaker. There was a wildness to the huge russet and olive slopes, sprinkled with giant boulders. Now and then we passed a moorland cottage. Each was walled and roofed with stone, with no plants to break its harsh outline. Suddenly we looked down into a cuplike depression. It was patched with stunted oaks and firs that had been twisted and bent by the fury of storms. Two high, narrow towers rose over the trees. The driver pointed with his whip. "Baskerville Hall," said he.

A few minutes later we had reached a maze of fantastic tracery in wrought iron. These were the lodge-gates, with weather-bitten pillars on either side, blotched with lichens, and marked by the boars' heads of the Baskervilles. The lodge was a ruin of black granite and bared ribs of rafters. But facing it was a new building, half constructed. This was to be the first fruit of Sir Charles's South African gold.

Through the gateway we passed into the avenue, where the wheels were again hushed amid the leaves, and the old trees shot their branches in a somber tunnel over our heads. Baskerville shuddered as he looked up the long, dark drive to where the house glimmered like a ghost at the farther end.

1. What is the setting of the passage? Include specific words and phrases from the scene in your answer.

____

____

2. How does the setting influence the overall tone of the passage? Use examples from the scene that demonstrate this relationship.

____

____

____

COMPLEXITY

LOW  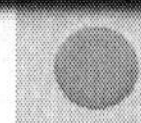  

Identifying the Setting Question Stems

Use these question stems to develop your own questions for students.

What is the setting of the text? Cite specific words and phrases from the text in your response.

What role does the setting play in the text? Include textual evidence to support your answer.

What is the historical significance of the setting of the text? Support your answer with textual examples.

Use textual details to describe the setting.

What impact would it have if the text occurred in a different location or time period? Provide textual evidence to illustrate your answer.

Describe the connection between the setting and character development. Support your answer with textual evidence.

What impact does the setting have on ______ (*character's*) life? Include specific details in your explanation.

Describe the connection between the setting and the theme. Support your answer with textual evidence.

What impact does the setting have on the text's overall tone? Use examples from the text that illustrate this relationship.

What exact words or phrases does the author use to describe the setting? Include textual evidence in your answer.

Name: ______________________________ Date: ______________

Excerpt from *The Adventures of Tom Sawyer*

Directions: Read this passage. Then, answer the questions.

The minister droned monotonously through a sermon so boring that many a head began to nod. Presently Tom remembered a treasure he had and got out a percussion-cap box. In it was an enormous black beetle with formidable jaws—a "pinchbug."

The beetle seized his finger; Tom shook his hand, and the beetle went floundering into the aisle and lit on its back, and the injured finger went into the boy's mouth. The beetle lay there working its legs helplessly, unable to turn over. Tom eyed it, and longed for it; but it was out of his reach. Other people uninterested in the sermon also eyed the pinchbug.

Presently a poodle came idling along and spied the beetle; his drooping tail lifted and wagged. He surveyed the prize; walked around it; smelled it from a safe distance; walked around it again; grew bolder, and took a closer smell; then lifted his lip and made a gingerly snatch at it, just missing it; made another, and another; laid down on his stomach with the beetle between his paws, and continued his experiments; grew weary at last, and then indifferent and absent-minded. His head nodded, and little by little his chin descended until it touched the enemy, who seized it. There was a sharp yelp, a jerk of the poodle's head, and the pinchbug fell a couple of yards away, on its back once more. Neighboring spectators shook with gentle inward laughter, several faces rapidly went behind fans and handkerchiefs, and Tom was entirely happy.

1. What role does the setting play in the passage? Include textual evidence to support your answer.

   ____

   ____

2. What exact words or phrases does the author use to describe the setting? Include textual evidence in your answer.

   ____

   ____

   ____

Identifying the Setting K–12 Alignment

Use this chart to determine the best question stems for your different groups of students.

☆	○	□	△
What is the setting?	Describe the setting. Use words and phrases from the text.	What is the setting of the text? Include specific words and phrases from the text in your answer.	What is the setting of the text? Cite specific words and phrases from the text in your response.
How does the setting affect the text? Give an example.	How does the setting influence the text? Give an example from the text.	What role does the setting play in the text? Include examples from the text to support your answer.	What role does the setting play in the text? Include textual evidence to support your answer.
Why is the time period of the text important? How do you know?	How does the time period influence the text? Use the text to explain.	What impact does the time period have on the text? Include a text example to support your answer.	What is the historical significance of the setting of the text? Support your answer with textual examples.
Tell what you know about the setting. Give details.	What do you know about the setting? Include details.	Use details from the text to describe the setting.	Use textual details to describe the setting.
How would the text change if it took place in a different place or time? Why?	How would the text change if it took place in a different place or time? Use the text to explain.	How would the text be different if it occurred in another time or place? Provide text evidence to support your answer.	What impact would it have if the text occurred in a different location or time period? Provide textual evidence to illustrate your answer.

Identifying the Setting K–12 Alignment *(cont.)*

★	●	■	▲
How is the setting related to ______ (*character*)? Why?	How does the setting relate to ______ (*character*)? Explain using examples from the text.	What is the connection between the setting and character development in the text? Support your answer with examples from the text.	Describe the connection between the setting and character development. Support your answer with textual evidence.
How does setting affect the life of ______ (*character*)? How do you know?	How is ______ (*character's*) life affected by the setting? Explain.	How is ______ (*character's*) life influenced by the setting? Give details in your explanation.	What impact does the setting have on ______ (*character's*) life? Include specific details in your explanation.
How does the text's setting relate to its theme? How do you know?	How does the setting of the text relate to its theme? Explain.	What is the connection between the setting and the theme? Support your answer with examples from the text.	Describe the connection between the setting and the theme. Support your answer with textual evidence.
How does the text's setting relate to its tone? Tell how you know.	How does the setting affect the overall tone of the text? Use examples from the text to describe this relationship.	How does the setting influence the overall tone of the text? Use examples from the text that demonstrate this relationship.	What impact does the setting have on the text's overall tone? Use examples from the text that illustrate this relationship.
What does the author tell you about the setting? Give an example.	How does the author describe the setting? Give an example.	How is the setting described? Use the text to explain your answer.	What exact words or phrases does the author use to describe the setting? Include textual evidence in your answer.

Understanding the Plot

Skill Overview

The plot is the sequence of events. It begins with a conflict, followed by rising action, culminates in a climax, and is followed by an ending, called a resolution. What's important is to help students understand the key events in the plot. In some novels, there are several simultaneous storylines that must be unraveled into separate plots.

The basis for every fiction plot is a conflict. It is the struggle that is the driving force of the story. A conflict may exist within one person, between two people, between people and society, or between people and the elements (nature). All the action is the result of this conflict. The climax is the "high" point, or turning point, which then leads to the resolution. When reading narrative nonfiction, you can see many of these same elements.

You can use a graphic organizer of an upside-down V to make a visual representation of almost any text's plot. The conflict is written at the left-side base, the rising action is written on the slope, the climax is written at the vertex, the falling action is written on the slope, and the resolution is written at the right-side base.

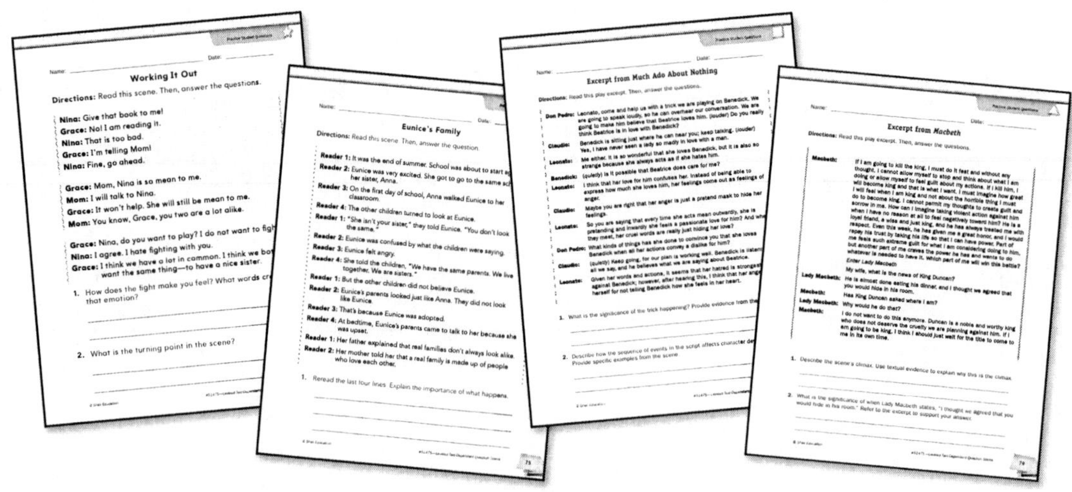

Implementing the Question Stems

This section includes 10 leveled, text-dependent question stems about understanding the plot. You can implement these question stems by connecting them to the fiction passages and/or nonfiction texts that you are reading in class.

It may seem as though using question stems would be easy, but it can be a complex task for teachers. To help you see how to implement these question stems in your classroom, this section includes student pages containing texts with sample text-dependent questions. Each of the four student pages illustrates a different complexity level.

Snapshot of Differentiating a Question

The chart below models how a single leveled question stem can be tied to both literature passages and informational texts at four complexity levels. This snapshot also gives you a quick view of how the question stems differ based on the complexity levels. However, you can also see how the question stems link to one another.

	Question Stem	Literature Example	Informational Text Example
☆	What words tell about ______ (*event*)? Why does it happen?	What words tell about Nate the Great's adventure? Why does it happen?	What words tell about Johnny Appleseed's decision to travel? Why does it happen?
○	Why is ______ (*event*) important? Explain using words from the text.	Why is the grandmother's visit important? Explain using words from the story.	Why is winning a court battle so important to Sojourner Truth? Use words from the text.
□	What is the significance of ______ happening? Provide evidence from the text.	What is the significance of the robbery? Provide evidence from the chapter.	What is the significance of the Mongolian invasion? Provide evidence from the text.
△	What is the significance of ______ (*event*)? Refer to the text to support your answer.	What is the significance of Mayella's accusations against Tom Robinson? Refer to the novel to support your answer.	What is the significance of the assassination of Archduke Franz Ferdinand? Refer to the text to support your answer.

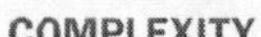

Understanding the Plot Question Stems

Use these question stems to develop your own questions for students.

How do the events on page ______ relate to those on page ______?

Why does the author have more than one person tell the text? How does this change the text?

What words tell about ______ (*event*)? Why does it happen?

Why does the author have ______ (*event*) happen? Use details from the text in your answer.

Tell how the events in the text affect the characters. Give an example.

What is the turning point in the text?

What happens right before ______ (*event*)? What happens right after ______ (*event*)?

Reread the page/paragraph that starts with ". . . ." What important thing happens?

What is the climax of the text? How do you know?

How does ______ (*event*) make you feel? What words create that emotion?

Name: ______________________ Date: __________

Working It Out

Directions: Read this scene. Then, answer the questions.

Nina: Give that book to me!

Grace: No! I am reading it.

Nina: That is too bad.

Grace: I'm telling Mom!

Nina: Fine, go ahead.

Grace: Mom, Nina is so mean to me.

Mom: I will talk to Nina.

Grace: It won't help. She will still be mean to me.

Mom: You know, Grace, you two are a lot alike.

Grace: Nina, do you want to play? I do not want to fight.

Nina: I agree. I hate fighting with you.

Grace: I think we have a lot in common. I think we both want the same thing—to have a nice sister.

1. How does the fight make you feel? What words create that emotion?

____

____

2. What is the turning point in the scene?

____

____

COMPLEXITY
LOW

Understanding the Plot Question Stems

Use these question stems to develop your own questions for students.

How do the events on page _____ relate to those on page _____? Give an example from the text.

Why does the author use more than one narrator? How does this change the text? Use the text in your explanation.

Why is _____ (*event*) important? Explain using words from the text.

Why does the author describe the _____ (*event*) so thoroughly? Use details from the text to answer.

How do the events in the text affect the characters? Use examples from the text.

How is _____ (*event*) a turning point in the text? Use details from the text in your answer.

What happens right before _____ (*event*)? What happens right after _____ (*event*)? Why is this series of events important?

Reread the page/paragraph that starts with ". . . ." Explain the importance of what happens.

Based on the events in the text, what is the climax? How do you know?

When _____ (*event*) takes place, how do you feel? What words does the author use to promote that feeling?

Name: ______________________________ Date: ______________

Eunice's Family

Directions: Read this scene. Then, answer the question.

Reader 1: It was the end of summer. School was about to start again.

Reader 2: Eunice was very excited. She got to go to the same school as her sister, Anna.

Reader 3: On the first day of school, Anna walked Eunice to her classroom.

Reader 4: The other children turned to look at Eunice.

Reader 1: "She isn't your sister," they told Eunice. "You don't look the same."

Reader 2: Eunice was confused by what the children were saying.

Reader 3: Eunice felt angry.

Reader 4: She told the children, "We have the same parents. We live together. We are sisters."

Reader 1: But the other children did not believe Eunice.

Reader 2: Eunice's parents looked just like Anna. They did not look like Eunice.

Reader 3: That's because Eunice was adopted.

Reader 4: At bedtime, Eunice's parents came to talk to her because she was upset.

Reader 1: Her father explained that real families don't always look alike.

Reader 2: Her mother told her that a real family is made up of people who love each other.

1. Reread the last four lines. Explain the importance of what happens.

____

____

____

COMPLEXITY

LOW    

Understanding the Plot Question Stems

Use these question stems to develop your own questions for students.

How do the events in chapter ______ affect those in chapter ______? Provide examples from the text.

Why does the author use flashbacks/foreshadowing/flash-forwards/multiple narrators? How does this affect the plot? Provide evidence from the text.

What is the significance of ______ (*event*) happening? Provide evidence from the text.

Why does the author focus on the events of ______? Use the text to support your response.

Describe how the sequence of events in the text affects character development. Provide specific examples from the text.

How does ______ (*event*) bring about a turning point? Provide evidence from the text.

What occurs prior to ______ (*event*)? What occurs after ______ (*event*)? Why is this sequence significant?

Reread the page/paragraph that starts with ". . . ." Describe the significant event that occurs.

Considering the events in the text, what is the climax? Use text evidence in your answer.

When ______ (*event*) occurs, how do you feel? What words does the author use to evoke that feeling?

Name: ______________________________ Date: ______________

Excerpt from *Much Ado About Nothing*

Directions: Read this play excerpt. Then, answer the questions.

Don Pedro: Leonato, come and help us with a trick we are playing on Benedick. We are going to speak loudly, so he can overhear our conversation. We are going to make him believe that Beatrice loves him. (*louder*) Do you really think Beatrice is in love with Benedick?

Claudio: Benedick is sitting just where he can hear you; keep talking. (*louder*) Yes, I have never seen a lady so madly in love with a man.

Leonato: Me either. It is so wonderful that she loves Benedick, but it is also so strange because she always acts as if she hates him.

Benedick: (*quietly*) Is it possible that Beatrice does care for me?

Leonato: I think that her love for him confuses her. Instead of being able to express how much she loves him, her feelings come out as feelings of anger.

Claudio: Maybe you are right that her anger is just a pretend mask to hide her feelings.

Leonato: So you are saying that every time she acts mean outwardly, she is pretending and inwardly she feels a passionate love for him? And when they meet, her cruel words are really just hiding her love?

Don Pedro: What kinds of things has she done to convince you that she loves Benedick when all her actions convey a dislike for him?

Claudio: (*quietly*) Keep going, for our plan is working well. Benedick is listening to all we say, and he believes what we are saying about Beatrice.

Leonato: Given her words and actions, it seems that her hatred is strongest against Benedick; however, after hearing this, I think that her anger is at herself for not telling Benedick how she feels in her heart.

1. What is the significance of the trick happening? Provide evidence from the scene.

____

____

2. Describe how the sequence of events in the script affects character development. Provide specific examples from the scene.

____

____

Understanding the Plot Question Stems

Use these question stems to develop your own questions for students.

Describe how the events in the text build on each other. Include specific examples from the text.

Why does the author use flashbacks/foreshadowing/flash-forwards/multiple narrators as a plot device? Justify your response with evidence from the text.

What is the significance of ______ (*event*)? Refer to the text to support your answer.

Why does the author emphasize the events of ______ (*event*)? Justify your answer with specific details from the text.

Explain the relationship between the sequence of events and character development in the text. Include specific examples from the text.

How does the event in paragraph ______ signify a turning point? Refer back to the text for details to support your answer.

What occurs prior to ______ (*event*)? What occurs after ______ (*event*)? Explain the significance of this sequence in the text.

Reread the page/paragraph that starts with ". . . . " Identify the significant event that occurs.

Describe the text's climax. Use textual evidence to explain why this is the climax.

How does the author build your emotions through the sequence of events? Include specific examples from the text to support your answer.

Name: ______________________________ Date: ______________

Excerpt from *Macbeth*

Directions: Read this play excerpt. Then, answer the questions.

Macbeth: If I am going to kill the king, I must do it fast and without any thought. I cannot allow myself to stop and think about what I am doing or allow myself to feel guilt about my actions. If I kill him, I will become king and that is what I want. I must imagine how great I will feel when I am king and not about the horrible thing I must do to become king. I cannot permit my thoughts to create guilt and sorrow in me. How can I imagine taking violent action against him when I have no reason at all to feel negatively toward him? He is a loyal friend, a wise and just king, and he has always treated me with respect. Even this week, he has given me a great honor, and I would repay his trust by taking his life so that I can have power. Part of me feels such extreme guilt for what I am considering doing to him, but another part of me craves the power he has and wants to do whatever is needed to have it. Which part of me will win this battle?

Enter Lady Macbeth

My wife, what is the news of King Duncan?

Lady Macbeth: He is almost done eating his dinner, and I thought we agreed that you would hide in his room.

Macbeth: Has King Duncan asked where I am?

Lady Macbeth: Why would he do that?

Macbeth: I do not want to do this anymore. Duncan is a noble and worthy king who does not deserve the cruelty we are planning against him. If I am going to be king, I think I should just wait for the title to come to me in its own time.

1. Describe the scene's climax. Use textual evidence to explain why this is the climax.

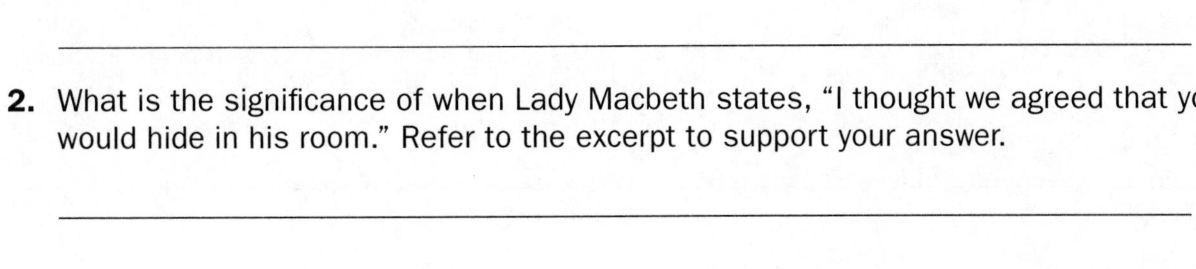

2. What is the significance of when Lady Macbeth states, "I thought we agreed that you would hide in his room." Refer to the excerpt to support your answer.

Understanding the Plot K–12 Alignment

Use this chart to determine the best question stems for your different groups of students.

☆	○	□	△
How do the events on page ______ relate to those on page ______?	How do the events on page ______ relate to those on page ______? Give an example from the text.	How do the events in chapter ______ affect those in chapter ______? Provide examples from the text.	Describe how the events in the text build on each other. Include specific examples from the text.
Why does the author have more than one person tell the text? How does this change the text?	Why does the author use more than one narrator? How does this change the text? Use the text in your explanation.	Why does the author use flashbacks/foreshadowing/flash-forwards/multiple narrators? How does this affect the plot? Provide evidence from the text.	Why does the author use flashbacks/foreshadowing/flash-forwards/multiple narrators as a plot device? Justify your response with evidence from the text.
What words tell about ______ (*event*)? Why does it happen?	Why is ______ (*event*) important? Explain using words from the text.	What is the significance of ______ (*event*) happening? Provide evidence from the text.	What is the significance of ______ (*event*)? Refer to the text to support your answer.
Why does the author have ______ (*event*) happen? Use details from the text in your answer.	Why does the author describe the ______ (*event*) so thoroughly? Use details from the text to answer.	Why does the author focus on the events of ______? Use the text to support your response.	Why does the author emphasize the events of ______ (*event*)? Justify your answer with specific details from the text.
Tell how the events in the text affect the characters. Give an example.	How do the events in the text affect the characters? Use examples from the text.	Describe how the sequence of events in the text affects character development. Provide specific examples from the text.	Explain the relationship between the sequence of events and character development in the text. Include specific examples from the text.

Understanding the Plot K–12 Alignment *(cont.)*

★	●	■	▲
What is the turning point in the text?	How is ______ *(event)* a turning point in the text? Use details from the text in your answer.	How does ______ (event) bring about a turning point? Provide evidence from the text.	How does the event in paragraph ______ signify a turning point? Refer back to the text for details to support your answer.
What happens right before ______ (*event*)? What happens right after ______ (*event*)?	What happens right before ______ (*event*)? What happens right after ______ (*event*)? Why is this series of events important?	What occurs prior to ______ (*event*)? What occurs after ______ (*event*)? Why is this sequence significant?	What occurs prior to ______ (*event*)? What occurs after ______ (*event*)? Explain the significance of this sequence in the text.
Reread the page/paragraph that starts with ". . . ." What important thing happens?	Reread the page/paragraph that starts with ". . . ." Explain the importance of what happens.	Reread the page/paragraph that starts with ". . . ." Describe the significant event that occurs.	Reread the page/paragraph that starts with ". . . . " Identify the significant event that occurs.
What is the climax of the text? How do you know?	Based on the events in the text, what is the climax? How do you know?	Considering the events in the text, what is the climax? Use text evidence in your answer.	Describe the text's climax. Use textual evidence to explain why this is the climax.
How does ______ (*event*) make you feel? What words create that emotion?	When ______ *(event)* takes place, how do you feel? What words does the author use to promote that feeling?	When ______ *(event)* occurs, how do you feel? What words does the author use to evoke that feeling?	How does the author build your emotions through the sequence of events? Include specific examples from the text to support your answer.

Analyzing Characters

Skill Overview

The ability to analyze characters helps students to comprehend the text as well as make accurate predictions about characters' goals and potential behaviors. Fictional characters often have a flaw that is important to the plot. It causes the characters to get into trouble or to learn life lessons.

The ability to analyze the people described in nonfiction texts is also an important skill. Many times, thinking about the personalitities of the people in nonfiction texts as well as the choices they make is just as vital to the comprehension of the texts as it is with fiction passages. (Throughout the question stems in this section, the term *character* is used. However, when using these question stems with narrative nonfiction, you may need to substitute the word *person* for the word *character.*)

Use a blank outline of a male or female (or an animal, if that is the protagonist) as a graphic organizer for character analysis. Use text-dependent questions to have students locate details in the text that tell about the character's personality. An author doesn't usually come right out and state what a character's personality is; the students must look at the character's actions and/or speech to discover clues to these traits. Have them write the clues they find from the text on the graphic organizer. Then, determine which traits the character has based on the evidence.

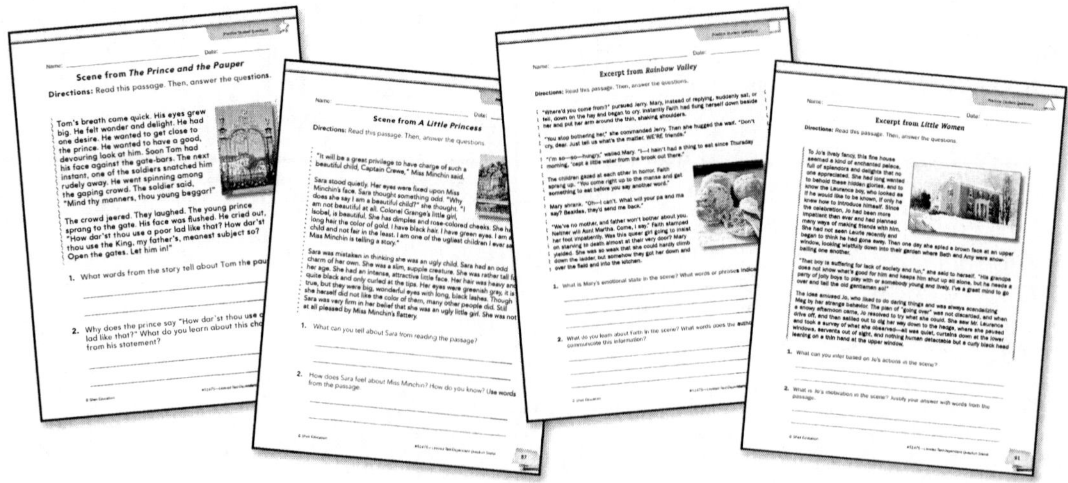

Implementing the Question Stems

This section includes 10 leveled, text-dependent question stems about analyzing characters. You can implement these question stems by connecting them to the fiction passages and/or nonfiction texts that you are reading in class.

It may seem as though using question stems would be easy, but it can be a complex task for teachers. To help you see how to implement these question stems in your classroom, this section includes student pages containing texts with sample text-dependent questions. Each of the four student pages illustrates a different complexity level.

Snapshot of Differentiating a Question

The chart below models how a single leveled question stem can be tied to both literature passages and informational texts at four complexity levels. This snapshot also gives you a quick view of how the question stems differ based on the complexity levels. However, you can also see how the question stems link to one another.

	Question Stem	Literature Example	Informational Text Example
☆	How does ______ change during the text? Give examples from the text.	How does Clifford change during the story? Give examples from the book.	How does Neil Armstrong change during the text? Give examples from the book.
○	How does ______ grow as a person? Support your answer with specific examples from the text.	How does Travis grow as a person? Support your answer with specific examples from the story.	How does Wilma Rudolph grow as a person? Support your answer with specific examples from the text.
□	How does the author show ______'s growth/change during the text? Use the text in your response.	How does the author show Hermione's growth/change during the novel? Use the text in your response.	How does the author show Gandhi's growth/change during the biography? Use the text in your response.
△	How does the author develop the character of ______ over the course of the text? Include specific examples from the text in your answer.	How does the author develop the character of Holden over the course of the novel? Include specific examples from the novel in your answer.	How does the author develop the character of Nelson Mandela over the course of the biography? Include specific examples from the text in your answer.

COMPLEXITY

LOW  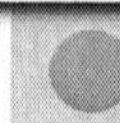 

Analyzing Characters Question Stems

Use these question stems to develop your own questions for students.

Who are the two main characters? How do you know they are the most important?

What words from the text tell about ______ (*character*)?

How does ______ (*character*) feel about ______ (*character*)? How do you know? Use words from the text.

What does ______ (*character*) do in page/paragraph ______? What does this let you know about ______ (*character*)?

How does ______ (*character*) act around ______ (*character*)? What does this tell you about their relationship?

What are ______ (*character's*) strengths? Weaknesses? How do you know?

Why does ______ (*character*) say ". . ."? What do you learn about this character from this statement?

How does ______ (*character*) feel in the ______ paragraph/page? What words in the text let you know this?

What problem does ______ (*character*) face? Use words from the text in your answer.

How does ______ (*character*) change during the text? Give examples from the text.

Name: ______________________ Date: ______________

Scene from *The Prince and the Pauper*

Directions: Read this passage. Then, answer the questions.

Tom's breath came quick. His eyes grew big. He felt wonder and delight. He had one desire. He wanted to get close to the prince. He wanted to have a good, devouring look at him. Soon Tom had his face against the gate-bars. The next instant, one of the soldiers snatched him rudely away. He went spinning among the gaping crowd. The soldier said, "Mind thy manners, thou young beggar!"

The crowd jeered. They laughed. The young prince sprang to the gate. His face was flushed. He cried out, "How dar'st thou use a poor lad like that? How dar'st thou use the King, my father's, meanest subject so? Open the gates. Let him in!"

1. What words from the story tell about Tom the pauper?

____

____

2. Why does the prince say "How dar'st thou use a poor lad like that?" What do you learn about this character from his statement?

____

____

COMPLEXITY

LOW

Analyzing Characters Question Stems

Use these question stems to develop your own questions for students.

Based on the events in the text, who are the main characters? Use details from the text in your answer.

What can you tell about ______ (*character*) from reading the ______ paragraph/page?

How does ______ (*character*) feel about ______ (*character*)? Use the text to tell how you know this.

What do ______ (*character's*) actions show you in the ______ page/paragraph? What can you tell about ______ (*character*) from these actions?

How does ______ (*character*) act around ______ (*character*)? What do these actions tell you about their relationship?

What does the author reveal about ______ (*character's*) strengths? Weaknesses? Use the text to explain.

How does the conversation between ______ (*character*) and ______ (*character*) help you learn more about these characters? Use examples from the text.

How does ______ (*character*) feel in the ______ paragraph/page? What words in the text tell you this?

What problems does ______ (*character*) face? How does his/her personality affect these problems? Use information from the text in your answer.

How does ______ (*character*) grow as a person? Support your answer with specific examples from the text.

Name: ______________________________ Date: ______________

Scene from *A Little Princess*

Directions: Read this passage. Then, answer the questions.

"It will be a great privilege to have charge of such a beautiful child, Captain Crewe," Miss Minchin said.

Sara stood quietly. Her eyes were fixed upon Miss Minchin's face. Sara thought something odd. "Why does she say I am a beautiful child?" she thought. "I am not beautiful at all. Colonel Grange's little girl, Isobel, is beautiful. She has dimples and rose-colored cheeks. She has long hair the color of gold. I have black hair. I have green eyes. I am a thin child and not fair in the least. I am one of the ugliest children I ever saw. Miss Minchin is telling a story."

Sara was mistaken in thinking she was an ugly child. Sara had an odd charm of her own. She was a slim, supple creature. She was rather tall for her age. She had an intense, attractive little face. Her hair was heavy and quite black and only curled at the tips. Her eyes were greenish gray, it is true, but they were big, wonderful eyes with long, black lashes. Though she herself did not like the color of them, many other people did. Still Sara was very firm in her belief that she was an ugly little girl. She was not at all pleased by Miss Minchin's flattery.

1. What can you tell about Sara from reading the passage?

____

____

2. How does Sara feel about Miss Minchin? How do you know? Use words from the passage.

____

____

COMPLEXITY

LOW   

Analyzing Characters Question Stems

Use these question stems to develop your own questions for students.

Since ______ (*character*) is not a main character, what is his/her role in the text? Why does the author include him/her? Use details from the text to prove your answer.

What do you learn about ______ (*character*) in the ______ paragraph/page? What words does the author use to communicate this information?

What are ______ (*character's*) feelings regarding ______ (*character*)? Use the text to explain.

What do ______ (*character's*) actions reveal in the ______ page/paragraph? What can you infer about ______ (*character*) from these actions?

How does ______ (*character*) behave when she/he is around ______ (*character*)? What does this tell you about their relationship?

What does the author want the reader to know/understand about ______ (*character's*) strengths and weaknesses? How do you know this from the text?

How does the dialogue between ______ (*character*) and ______ (*character*) help to develop these characters? How does this dialogue relate to ______ (*character's*) personality? Provide examples.

What is ______ (*character's*) motivation/emotional state in the ______ paragraph/scene? What words or phrases indicate this?

What problems does ______ (*character*) face? How does his/her personality affect the outcome of these problems? Use examples from the text in your answer.

How does the author show ______ (*character's*) growth/change during the text? Use the text in your response.

Name: ______________________________ Date: ______________

Excerpt from *Rainbow Valley*

Directions: Read this passage. Then, answer the questions.

"Where'd you come from?" pursued Jerry. Mary, instead of replying, suddenly sat, or fell, down on the hay and began to cry. Instantly Faith had flung herself down beside her and put her arm around the thin, shaking shoulders.

"You stop bothering her," she commanded Jerry. Then she hugged the waif. "Don't cry, dear. Just tell us what's the matter. WE'RE friends."

"I'm so—so—hungry," wailed Mary. "I—I hain't had a thing to eat since Thursday morning, 'cept a little water from the brook out there."

The children gazed at each other in horror. Faith sprang up. "You come right up to the manse and get something to eat before you say another word."

Mary shrank. "Oh—I can't. What will your pa and ma say? Besides, they'd send me back."

"We've no mother, and father won't bother about you. Neither will Aunt Martha. Come, I say." Faith stamped her foot impatiently. Was this queer girl going to insist on starving to death almost at their very door? Mary yielded. She was so weak that she could hardly climb down the ladder, but somehow they got her down and over the field and into the kitchen.

1. What is Mary's emotional state in the scene? What words or phrases indicate this?

____

____

____

2. What do you learn about Faith in the scene? What words does the author use to communicate this information?

____

____

____

COMPLEXITY

LOW    

Analyzing Characters Question Stems

Use these question stems to develop your own questions for students.

- Since ______ (*character*) is not a main character, why does the author choose to include him/her? Support your answer with textual evidence.
- In the ______ paragraph/page, you learn more about ______ (*character*). What can you infer from this? Use the text to support your response.
- What emotions does ______ (*character*) experience? Include evidence from the text to support your answer.
- What can you infer based on ______ (*character's*) actions in the ______ page/paragraph?
- What is the relationship between ______ (*character*) and ______ (*character*)? Refer back to the text for specific examples to support your answer.
- The author includes details about ______ (*character's*) strengths and weaknesses. Why? Justify your answer using the text to provide evidence.
- How does the dialogue between ______ (*character*) and ______ (*character*) help to develop both characters? How does this dialogue give you a new perspective on ______ (*character's*) personality? Use details from the text in your response.
- What is ______ (*character's*) motivation/emotional state in the ______ paragraph/page? Justify your answer with words from the text.
- What problems does ______ (*character*) encounter? How does his/her personality affect the resolution of these problems? Use textual evidence in your answer.
- How does the author develop the character of ______ (*character*) over the course of the text? Include specific examples from the text in your answer.

Name: ______________________________ Date: ______________

Excerpt from *Little Women*

Directions: Read this passage. Then, answer the questions.

To Jo's lively fancy, this fine house seemed a kind of enchanted palace, full of splendors and delights that no one appreciated. She had long wanted to behold these hidden glories, and to know the Laurence boy, who looked as if he would like to be known, if only he knew how to introduce himself. Since the celebration, Jo had been more impatient than ever and had planned many ways of making friends with him. She had not seen Laurie recently and began to think he had gone away. Then one day she spied a brown face at an upper window, looking wistfully down into their garden where Beth and Amy were snow-balling one another.

"That boy is suffering for lack of society and fun," she said to herself. "His grandpa does not know what's good for him and keeps him shut up all alone, but he needs a party of jolly boys to play with or somebody young and lively. I've a great mind to go over and tell the old gentleman so!"

The idea amused Jo, who liked to do daring things and was always scandalizing Meg by her strange behavior. The plan of "going over" was not discarded, and when a snowy afternoon came, Jo resolved to try what she could. She saw Mr. Laurence drive off, and then sallied out to dig her way down to the hedge, where she paused and took a survey of what she observed—all was quiet, curtains down at the lower windows, servants out of sight, and nothing human detectable but a curly black head leaning on a thin hand at the upper window.

1. What can you infer based on Jo's actions in the scene?

____

____

2. What is Jo's motivation in the scene? Justify your answer with words from the passage.

____

____

Analyzing Characters K–12 Alignment

Use this chart to determine the best question stems for your different groups of students.

☆	○	□	△
Who are the two main characters? How do you know they are the most important?	Based on the events in the text, who are the main characters? Use details from the text in your answer.	Since ______ (*character*) is not a main character, what is his/her role in the text? Why does the author include him/her? Use details from the text to prove your answer.	Since ______ (*character*) is not a main character, why does the author choose to include him/her? Support your answer with textual evidence.
What words from the text tell about ______ (*character*)?	What can you tell about ______ (*character*) from reading the ______ paragraph/page?	What do you learn about ______ (*character*) in the ______ paragraph/scene? What words does the author use to communicate this information?	In the ______ paragraph/page, you learn more about ______ (*character*). What can you infer from this? Use the text to support your response.
How does ______ (*character*) feel about ______ (*character*)? How do you know? Use words from the text.	How does ______ (*character*) feel about ______ (*character*)? Use the text to tell how you know this.	What are ______ (*character's*) feelings regarding ______ (*character*)? Use the text to explain.	What emotions does ______ (*character*) experience? Include evidence from the text to support your answer.
What does ______ (*character*) do in page/paragraph ______? What does this let you know about ______ (*character*)?	What do ______ (*character's*) actions show you in the ______ page/paragraph? What can you tell about ______ (*character*) from these actions?	What do ______ (*character's*) actions reveal in the ______ page/paragraph? What can you infer about ______ (*character*) from these actions?	What can you infer based on ______ (*character's*) actions in the ______ page/paragraph?
How does ______ (*character*) act around ______ (*character*)? What does this tell you about their relationship?	How does ______ (*character*) act around ______ (*character*)? What do these actions tell you about their relationship?	How does ______ (*character*) behave when she/he is around ______ (*character*)? What does this tell you about their relationship?	What is the relationship between ______ (*character*) and ______ (*character*)? Refer back to the text for specific examples to support your answer.

Analyzing Characters K–12 Alignment *(cont.)*

☆	○	□	△
What are ______ (*character's*) strengths? Weaknesses? How do you know?	What does the author reveal about ______ (*character's*) strengths? Weaknesses? Use the text to explain.	What does the author want the reader to know/understand about ______ (*character's*) strengths and weaknesses? How do you know this from the text?	The author includes details about ______ (*character's*) strengths and weaknesses. Why? Justify your answer using the text to provide evidence.
Why does ______ (*character*) say ". . ."? What do you learn about this character from this statement?	How does the conversation between ______ (*character*) and ______ (*character*) help you learn more about these characters? Use examples from the text.	How does the dialogue between ______ (*character*) and ______ (*character*) help to develop these characters? How does this dialogue relate to ______ (*character's*) personality? Provide examples.	How does the dialogue between ______ (*character*) and ______ (*character*) help to develop both characters? How does this dialogue give you a new perspective on ______ (*character's*) personality? Use details from the text in your response.
How does ______ (*character*) feel in the ______ paragraph/page? What words in the text let you know this?	How does ______ (*character*) feel in the ______ paragraph/page? What words in the text tell you this?	What is ______ (*character's*) motivation/emotional state in the ______ paragraph/scene? What words or phrases indicate this?	What is ______ (*character's*) motivation/emotional state in the ______ paragraph/scene? Justify your answer with words from the text.
What problem does ______ (*character*) face? Use words from the text in your answer.	What problems does ______ (*character*) face? How does his/her personality affect these problems? Use information from the text in your answer.	What problems does ______ (*character*) face? How does his/her personality affect the outcome of these problems? Use examples from the text in your answer.	What problems does ______ (*character*) encounter? How does his/her personality affect the resolution of these problems? Use textual evidence in your answer.
How does ______ (*character*) change during the text? Give examples from the text.	How does ______ (*character*) grow as a person? Support your answer with specific examples from the text.	How does the author show ______ (*character's*) growth/change during the text? Use the text in your response.	How does the author develop the character of ______ (*character*) over the course of the text? Include specific examples from the text in your answer.

Analyzing Text Structure

Skill Overview

Structure is the way in which the various elements of a text are assembled. This includes the voice in which the text is told and the organization of the text. While classic literature is usually written in third person with a detached narrator, most modern fiction is written in first person through the eyes of a character. To keep readers turning the page, authors may use:

- **flash-forwards**—interrupting scenes that are set in a later time than the primary text
- **flashbacks**—interrupting scenes that are set in an earlier time than the main text
- **foreshadowing**—a warning or implication of events that will occur later in the text
- **plot twists**—a shocking change in a character's behavior or the expected outcome of the plot

Skillful readers use text structure to construct meaning. Use text-dependent questions to help your students to analyze text structure.

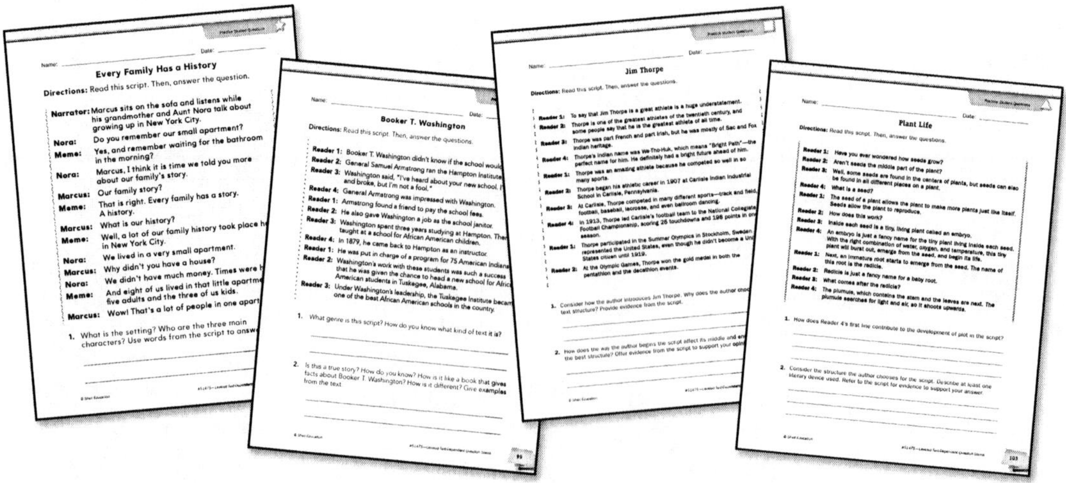

Implementing the Question Stems

This section includes 10 leveled, text-dependent question stems about analyzing text structure. You can implement these question stems by connecting them to the fiction passages and/or nonfiction texts that you are reading in class.

It may seem as though using question stems would be easy, but it can be a complex task for teachers. To help you see how to implement these question stems in your classroom, this section includes student pages containing texts with sample text-dependent questions. Each of the four student pages illustrates a different complexity level.

Snapshot of Differentiating a Question

The chart below models how a single leveled question stem can be tied to both literature passages and informational texts at four complexity levels. This snapshot also gives you a quick view of how the question stems differ based on the complexity levels. However, you can also see how the question stems link to one another.

	Question Stem	Literature Example	Informational Text Example
☆	Does this text tell a story or give information? How do you know?	Does *The Little Red Hen* tell a story or give information? How do you know?	Does *Chicks and Chickens* tell a story or give information? How do you know?
○	Is this a true story? How do you know? How is it like a book that gives facts about _______? How is it different? Give examples from the text.	Is this a true story? How do you know? How is it like a book that gives facts about the Statue of Liberty? How is it different? Give examples from the text.	Is this a true story? How do you know? How is it like a book that tells a story about the first Thanksgiving? How is it different? Give examples from the text.
□	How does this text differ from one that gives information about _______? Refer to specific aspects of the text in your answer.	How does this book differ from one that gives information about sea turtles? Refer to specific aspects of the book in your answer.	How does this text differ from one that tells a story about carnivorous plants? Refer to specific aspects of the text in your answer.
△	Is this a work of fiction or nonfiction? How does this book differ from a book that provides facts about _______? Give specific examples from the text.	Is this a work of fiction or nonfiction? How does this novel differ from a book that provides facts about the French Revolution? Give specific examples from the text.	Is this a work of fiction or nonfiction? How does this book differ from historical fiction about Japanese immigrants? Give specific examples from the text.

COMPLEXITY

LOW  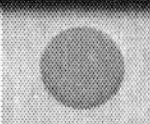 

Analyzing Text Structure Question Stems

Use these question stems to develop your own questions for students.

- Could this text really happen? How do you know?
- Does this text tell a story or give information? How do you know?
- What words in the text do the characters speak? How do you know?
- What happens in the beginning? The middle? The end?
- What is the setting? Who are the two main characters? Use words from the text to answer.
- What is the main problem in the text? Why isn't it presented right away?
- Who is telling the text/story? How would the text change if someone else told it?
- How does the _____ sentence on page _____ add to the plot?
- What happens first? Next? Then? Why is this order of events important?
- Reread the start of the text. Why does the author begin the text this way?

Name: ______________________________ Date: ______________

Every Family Has a History

Directions: Read this script. Then, answer the question.

Narrator: Marcus sits on the sofa and listens while his grandmother and Aunt Nora talk about growing up in New York City.

Nora: Do you remember our small apartment?

Meme: Yes, and remember waiting for the bathroom in the morning?

Nora: Marcus, I think it is time we told you more about our family's story.

Marcus: Our family story?

Meme: That is right. Every family has a story. A history.

Marcus: What is our history?

Meme: Well, a lot of our family history took place here in New York City.

Nora: We lived in a very small apartment.

Marcus: Why didn't you have a house?

Nora: We didn't have much money. Times were hard.

Meme: And eight of us lived in that little apartment—five adults and the three of us kids.

Marcus: Wow! That's a lot of people in one apartment.

1. What is the setting? Who are the three main characters? Use words from the script to answer.

____

____

COMPLEXITY

LOW  

Analyzing Text Structure Question Stems

Use these question stems to develop your own questions for students.

What genre is this text? How do you know what kind of text it is?

Is this a true story? How do you know? How is it like a book that gives facts about ______? How is it different? Give examples from the text.

Why does the author include conversations in the text? How does this help the text? Give examples from the text.

How does the way the author begins the text affect its middle? Its end? Is this a good structure? Support your answer with details from the text.

Based on the events in the text, who are the two main characters? What is the setting? Use the text to explain.

Why does the author build up to the text's main problem? How does that affect the text? Use the text to explain.

How does the author structure the text? Why does the author do this? Use the text to support your answer.

What is the plot twist that occurs in this part of the text? Explain.

Think of the sequence of events. Why does the author choose this order for the plot?

Reread the first ______ sentences. What is their purpose? Why does the author choose to start with these events? Use examples from the text.

Name: ______________________________ Date: ______________

Booker T. Washington

Directions: Read this script. Then, answer the questions.

Reader 1: Booker T. Washington didn't know if the school would let him in.

Reader 2: General Samuel Armstrong ran the Hampton Institute.

Reader 3: Washington said, "I've heard about your new school. I'm hungry and broke, but I'm not a fool."

Reader 4: General Armstrong was impressed with Washington.

Reader 1: Armstrong found a friend to pay the school fees.

Reader 2: He also gave Washington a job as the school janitor.

Reader 3: Washington spent three years studying at Hampton. Then he taught at a school for African American children.

Reader 4: In 1879, he came back to Hampton as an instructor.

Reader 1: He was put in charge of a program for 75 American Indians.

Reader 2: Washington's work with these students was such a success that he was given the chance to head a new school for African American students in Tuskegee, Alabama.

Reader 3: Under Washington's leadership, the Tuskegee Institute became one of the best African American schools in the country.

1. What genre is this script? How do you know what kind of text it is?

____

____

2. Is this a true story? How do you know? How is it like a book that gives facts about Booker T. Washington? How is it different? Give examples from the text.

____

____

____

COMPLEXITY

LOW

Analyzing Text Structure Question Stems

Use these question stems to develop your own questions for students.

What is the text's genre? How is it helpful for the reader to understand the genre?

How does this text differ from one that gives information about ______? Refer to specific aspects of the text in your answer.

How does the author use dialogue in the text? What effect does the dialogue have? Provide examples from the text.

How does the way the author begins the text affect its middle and ending? Is this the best structure? Offer evidence from the text to support your opinion.

Consider how the author introduces the setting and characters. Why does the author choose this text structure? Provide evidence from the text.

Why does the author delay in introducing the text's major conflict? How does this timing affect the text's structure? Support your answer using the text.

Think about the structure the author uses in the text. What literary device is used? Use the text to support your answer.

How does the ______ sentence on page ______ keep the plot moving forward? Explain.

How does the author use time in the text? How does this affect the reader? Support your answer with evidence from the text.

Reread the first ______ sentences of the text. What is the purpose of these sentences? Why does the author choose to begin this way? Support your answer with examples from the text.

Name: ______________________________ Date: ____________

Jim Thorpe

Directions: Read this script. Then, answer the questions.

Reader 1: To say that Jim Thorpe is a great athlete is a huge understatement.

Reader 2: Thorpe is one of the greatest athletes of the twentieth century, and some people say that he is the greatest athlete of all time.

Reader 3: Thorpe was part French and part Irish, but he was mostly of Sac and Fox Indian heritage.

Reader 4: Thorpe's Indian name was Wa-Tho-Huk, which means "Bright Path"—the perfect name for him. He definitely had a bright future ahead of him.

Reader 1: Thorpe was an amazing athlete because he competed so well in so many sports.

Reader 2: Thorpe began his athletic career in 1907 at Carlisle Indian Industrial School in Carlisle, Pennsylvania.

Reader 3: At Carlisle, Thorpe competed in many different sports—track and field, football, baseball, lacrosse, and even ballroom dancing.

Reader 4: In 1913, Thorpe led Carlisle's football team to the National Collegiate Football Championship, scoring 25 touchdowns and 198 points in one season.

Reader 1: Thorpe participated in the Summer Olympics in Stockholm, Sweden. He represented the United States, even though he didn't become a United States citizen until 1919.

Reader 2: At the Olympic Games, Thorpe won the gold medal in both the pentathlon and the decathlon events.

1. Consider how the author introduces Jim Thorpe. Why does the author choose this text structure? Provide evidence from the script.

____

____

2. How does the way the author begins the script affect its middle and ending? Is this the best structure? Offer evidence from the script to support your opinion.

____

____

COMPLEXITY

LOW

Analyzing Text Structure Question Stems

Use these question stems to develop your own questions for students.

What is the text's genre? For what reasons is it important for the reader to understand the genre?

Is this a work of fiction or nonfiction? How does this text differ from a text that provides facts about ______? Give specific examples from the text.

How does the author use dialogue and what effect does it have on the text? Justify your answer with textual evidence.

How does the way the author begins the text affect its middle and ending? Is this a good structure? Can it be improved? Cite the text to support your answer.

How and when does the author introduce the reader to the setting and characters in the text? Why does the author utilize this text structure? Include textual evidence.

Why does the author choose to delay the introduction of the text's major conflict? How does this timing affect the text's structure? Use specific examples from the text.

Consider the structure the author chooses for the text. Describe at least one literary device used. Refer to the text for evidence to support your answer.

How does the ______ sentence on page ______ contribute to the development of plot in the text?

How does the author manipulate time in the text? What effect does this have for the reader? Provide evidence from the text.

Reread the first ______ sentences of the text to determine their purpose. Why does the author choose to start the text with these events? Provide specific evidence from the text.

Name: ______________________________ Date: ____________

Plant Life

Directions: Read this script. Then, answer the questions.

Reader 1: Have you ever wondered how seeds grow?

Reader 2: Aren't seeds the middle part of the plant?

Reader 3: Well, some seeds are found in the centers of plants, but seeds can also be found in all different places on a plant.

Reader 4: What is a seed?

Reader 1: The seed of a plant allows the plant to make more plants just like itself. Seeds allow the plant to reproduce.

Reader 2: How does this work?

Reader 3: Inside each seed is a tiny, living plant called an embryo.

Reader 4: An embryo is just a fancy name for the tiny plant living inside each seed. With the right combination of water, oxygen, and temperature, this tiny plant will burst out, emerge from the seed, and begin its life.

Reader 1: Next, an immature root starts to emerge from the seed. The name of this root is the radicle.

Reader 2: Radicle is just a fancy name for a baby root.

Reader 3: What comes after the radicle?

Reader 4: The plumule, which contains the stem and the leaves are next. The plumule searches for light and air, so it shoots upwards.

1. How does Reader 4's first line contribute to the development of plot in the script?

____

____

____

2. Consider the structure the author chooses for the script. Describe at least one literary device used. Refer to the script for evidence to support your answer.

____

____

____

Analyzing Text Structure K–12 Alignment

Use this chart to determine the best question stems for your different groups of students.

☆	○	□	△
Could this text really happen? How do you know?	What genre is this text? How do you know what kind of text it is?	What is the text's genre? How is it helpful for the reader to understand the genre?	What is the text's genre? For what reasons is it important for the reader to understand the genre?
Does this text tell a story or give information? How do you know?	Is this a true story? How do you know? How is it like a book that gives facts about ______? How is it different? Give examples from the text.	How does this text differ from one that gives information about ______? Refer to specific aspects of the text in your answer.	Is this a work of fiction or nonfiction? How does this text differ from a text that provides facts about ______? Give specific examples from the text.
What words in the text do the characters speak? How do you know?	Why does the author include conversations in the text? How does this help the text? Give examples from the text.	How does the author use dialogue in the text? What effect does the dialogue have? Provide examples from the text.	How does the author use dialogue and what effect does it have on the text? Justify your answer with textual evidence.
What happens in the beginning? The middle? The end?	How does the way the author begins the text affect its middle? Its end? Is this a good structure? Support your answer with details from the text.	How does the way the author begins the text affect its middle and ending? Is this the best structure? Offer evidence from the text to support your opinion.	How does the way the author begins the text affect its middle and ending? Is this a good structure? Could it be improved? Cite the text to support your answer.
What is the setting? Who are the two main characters? Use words from the text to answer.	Based on the events in the text, who are the two main characters? What is the setting? Use the text to explain.	Consider how the author introduces the setting and characters. Why does the author choose this text structure? Provide evidence from the text.	How and when does the author introduce the reader to the setting and characters in the text? Why does the author utilize this text structure? Include textual evidence.

Analyzing Text Structure K–12 Alignment *(cont.)*

☆	○	□	△
What is the main problem in the text? Why isn't it presented right away?	Why does the author build up to the text's main problem? How does that affect the text? Use the text to explain.	Why does the author delay in introducing the text's major conflict? How does this timing affect the text's structure? Support your answer using the text.	Why does the author choose to delay the introduction of the text's major conflict? How does this timing affect the text's structure? Use specific examples from the text.
Who is telling the text/story? How would the text change if someone else told it?	How does the author structure the text? Why does the author do this? Use the text to support your answer.	Think about the structure the author uses in the text. What literary device is used? Use the text to support your answer.	Consider the structure the author chooses for the text. Describe at least one literary device used. Refer to the text for evidence to support your answer.
How does the ______ sentence on page ______ add to the plot?	What is the plot twist that occurs in this part of the text? Explain.	How does the ______ sentence on page ______ keep the plot moving forward? Explain.	How does the ______ sentence on page ______ contribute to the development of plot in the text?
What happens first? Next? Then? Why is this order of events important?	Think of the sequence of events. Why does the author choose this order for the plot?	How does the author use time in the text? How does this affect the reader? Support your answer with evidence from the text.	How does the author manipulate time in the text? What effect does this have for the reader? Provide evidence from the text.
Reread the start of the text. Why does the author begin the text this way?	Reread the first ______ sentences. What is their purpose? Why does the author choose to start with these events? Use examples from the text.	Reread the first ______ sentences of the text. What is the purpose of these sentences? Why does the author choose to begin this way? Support your answer with examples from the text.	Reread the first ______ sentences of the text to determine their purpose. Why does the author choose to start the text with these events? Provide specific evidence from the text.

Identifying Point of View

Skill Overview

Authors write fiction to entertain; the more interesting and believable the characters they create, the more memorable the book. For a character to have depth, he or she must have a point of view.

Authors write nonfiction to inform, to entertain, or to persuade. As a result, observant readers consider the source of information and expect to see proof to support the author's reasoning. Readers pay attention to conflicting accounts and connotative language.

Point of view text-dependent questions call students' attention to the phrases and sentences in the text containing clues to the characters' or writer's viewpoints. They help students to hone in on which words make the point of view clear, even if it's not directly stated. In this way, text-dependent questions help students notice differing points of view, explain why they occur, and examine the author's purpose in writing the text.

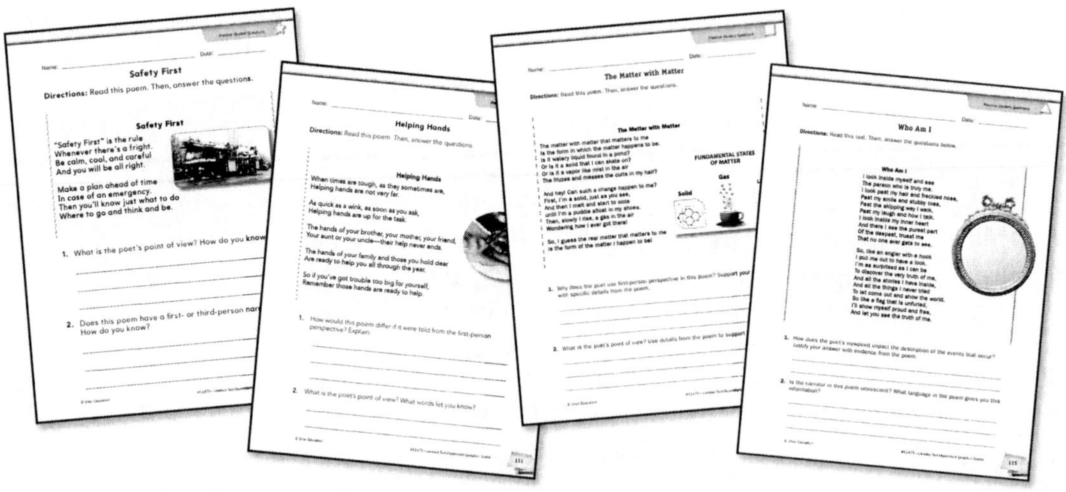

Implementing the Question Stems

This section includes 10 leveled, text-dependent question stems about identifying point of view. You can implement these question stems by connecting them to the fiction passages and/or nonfiction texts that you are reading in class.

It may seem as though using question stems would be easy, but it can be a complex task for teachers. To help you see how to implement these question stems in your classroom, this section includes student pages containing texts with sample text-dependent questions. Each of the four student pages illustrates a different complexity level.

Snapshot of Differentiating a Question

The chart below models how a single leveled question stem can be tied to both literature passages and informational texts at four complexity levels. This snapshot also gives you a quick view of how the question stems differ based on the complexity levels. However, you can also see how the question stems link to one another.

	Question Stem	Literature Example	Informational Text Example
☆	What is ______'s point of view? How do you know?	What is Little Bear's point of view? How do you know?	What is the scientist's point of view? How do you know?
○	How does ______ (*character*)'s point of view differ from ______ (*character*)'s point of view? Support your answer with examples from the text.	How does Charlotte's point of view differ from Templeton's point of view? Support your answer with examples from the book.	How does the farmer's point of view differ from the migrant worker's point of view? Support your answer with examples from the text.
□	What is the point of view of each character? Use specific words and phrases from the text to support your answer.	What is the point of view of each character in *The Westing Game*? Use specific words and phrases from the novel to support your answer.	What is the point of view of each person quoted in the debate? Use specific words and phrases from the text to support your answer.
△	Describe the different points of view of each character. Cite textual evidence.	Describe the different points of view of Huck and Jim. Cite textual evidence.	Describe the different points of view of Roosevelt and Churchill. Cite textual evidence.

COMPLEXITY

LOW   

Identifying Point of View Question Stems

Use these question stems to develop your own questions for students.

Who is telling the text? How do you know?

What is ______ (*character's*) point of view? How do you know?

What is ______ (*first character's*) point of view? What is ______ (*second character's*) point of view? How are they different?

How do ______ (*character's*) words/actions let us know his/her viewpoint? Use the text to explain.

Does this text have a first- or third-person narrator? How do you know?

How does ______ (*character's*) attitude affect the problem in the text?

How does the author/narrator feel about ______ (*character*)? How do you know?

How is ______ (*character's*) viewpoint shown through conversation? Explain.

How does the author's/narrator's opinion affect how the events are told? Give an example.

What culture does this text come from? How does that affect how the text is told?

Name: ______________________ Date: ____________

Safety First

Directions: Read this poem. Then, answer the questions.

Safety First

"Safety First" is the rule
Whenever there's a fright.
Be calm, cool, and careful
And you will be all right.

Make a plan ahead of time
In case of an emergency.
Then you'll know just what to do
Where to go and think and be.

1. What is the poet's point of view? How do you know?

____

____

____

2. Does this poem have a first- or third-person narrator? How do you know?

____

____

____

COMPLEXITY

LOW

Identifying Point of View Question Stems

Use these question stems to develop your own questions for students.

How many different narrators are in the text? Use text examples to show how you know this information.

How does ______ (*character's*) point of view differ from ______ (*character's*) point of view? Support your answer with examples from the text.

How does the author use point of view to help the reader learn about the characters/people? Use the text to explain.

How does the author show the point of view of ______ (*character*) over the course of the text? Use the text to explain.

How would this text differ if it were told from the first-/third-person perspective? Explain.

Based on the events in the text, how does ______ (*character's*) attitude cause/create/affect the problem? Use details from the text in your answer.

What is the author's/narrator's point of view? What words let you know?

How is ______ (*character's*) viewpoint revealed through the conversations he/she has? Use the text to tell how you know.

How does the author's/narrator's point of view influence how the events are explained? Use the text to prove your answer.

What culture does this text come from? How does it affect the development of the text?

Name: ______________________________ Date: ______________

Helping Hands

Directions: Read this poem. Then, answer the questions.

Helping Hands

When times are tough, as they sometimes are,
Helping hands are not very far.

As quick as a wink, as soon as you ask,
Helping hands are up for the task.

The hands of your brother, your mother, your friend,
Your aunt or your uncle—their help never ends.

The hands of your family and those you hold dear
Are ready to help you all through the year.

So if you've got trouble too big for yourself,
Remember those hands are ready to help.

1. How would this poem differ if it were told from the first-person perspective? Explain.

____

____

____

2. What is the poet's point of view? What words let you know?

____

____

Identifying Point of View Question Stems

Use these question stems to develop your own questions for students.

Why does the author choose to have multiple narrators? Use information from the text to support your response.

What is the point of view of each character? Use specific words and phrases from the text to support your answer.

Use details from the text to show how the author uses different viewpoints to develop the characters.

How does the author develop ______ (*character's*) point of view through his/her speech and behavior? Use specific words and phrases from the text to support your answer.

Why does the author use first-/third-person perspective in this text? Support your answer with specific details from the text.

How do the characters' opinions add to the conflict and its resolution? Explain your answer using examples from the text.

What is the author's/narrator's point of view? Use details from the text to support your answer.

How is ______ (*character's*) viewpoint expressed through the dialogue in the text? Use specific lines from the text to prove your answer.

How does the author's/narrator's point of view influence the description of the events that occur? Provide evidence from the text to support your answer.

Explain how the culture this text comes from influences the way the text is told.

Name: ______________________________ Date: ______________

The Matter with Matter

Directions: Read this poem. Then, answer the questions.

The Matter with Matter

The matter with matter that matters to me
Is the form in which the matter happens to be.
Is it watery liquid found in a pond?
Or is it a solid that I can skate on?
Or is it a vapor like mist in the air
The frizzes and messes the curls in my hair?

And hey! Can such a change happen to me?
First, I'm a solid, just as you see,
And then I melt and start to ooze
until I'm a puddle afloat in my shoes.
Then, slowly I rise, a gas in the air
Wondering how I ever got there!

So, I guess the real matter that matters to me
Is the form of the matter *I* happen to be!

FUNDAMENTAL STATES OF MATTER

Solid

Gas

Liquid

1. Why does the poet use first-person perspective in this poem? Support your answer with specific details from the poem.

____

____

____

2. What is the poet's point of view? Use details from the poem to support your answer.

____

____

____

COMPLEXITY

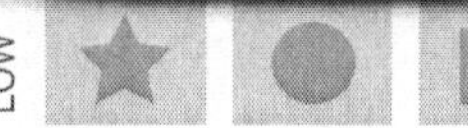

Identifying Point of View Question Stems

Use these question stems to develop your own questions for students.

Why do you think the author has multiple narrators? Support your answer with evidence from the text.

Describe the different points of view of each character. Cite textual evidence.

How does the author use different viewpoints to enhance the development of the characters? Justify your response with evidence from the text.

How does the author develop ______ (*character's*) point of view without explicitly stating it in the text? Include text evidence in your response.

Is the narrator in this text omniscient? What language in the text gives you this information?

How do the characters' points of view contribute to the conflict and its resolution in the text? Justify your answer with text evidence.

What is the author's/narrator's viewpoint regarding ______ (*character*)? Provide evidence from the text to support your answer.

How is ______ (*character's*) viewpoint expressed through the dialogue in the text? Include specific quotes from the text.

How does the author's/narrator's viewpoint impact the description of the events that occur? Justify your answer with evidence from the text.

Explain how the culture this text comes from has an impact on the text. How would the text differ if it were told from a different cultural viewpoint?

Name: ______________________________ Date: ______________

Who Am I

Directions: Read this text. Then, answer the questions below.

Who Am I

I look inside myself and see
The person who is truly me.
I look past my hair and freckled nose,
Past my smile and stubby toes,
Past the skipping way I walk,
Past my laugh and how I talk.
I look inside my inner heart
And there I see the purest part
Of the deepest, truest me
That no one ever gets to see.

So, like an angler with a hook
I pull *me* out to have a look.
I'm as surprised as I can be
To discover the very truth of me,
And all the stories I have inside,
And all the things I never tried
To let come out and show the world.
So like a flag that is unfurled,
I'll show myself proud and free,
And let you see the truth of me.

1. How does the poet's viewpoint impact the description of the events that occur? Justify your answer with evidence from the poem.

____

____

2. Is the narrator in this poem omniscient? What language in the poem gives you this information?

____

____

____

Identifying Point of View K–12 Alignment

Use this chart to determine the best question stems for your different groups of students.

☆	○	□	△
Who is telling the text? How do you know?	How many different narrators are in the text? Use text examples to show how you know this information.	Why does the author choose to have multiple narrators? Use information from the text to support your response.	Why do you think the author has multiple narrators? Support your answer with evidence from the text.
What is ______ (*character's*) point of view? How do you know?	How does ______ (*character's*) point of view differ from ______ (*character's*) point of view? Support your answer with examples from the text.	What is the point of view of each character? Use specific words and phrases from the text to support your answer.	Describe the different points of view of each character. Cite textual evidence.
What is ______ (*first character's*) point of view? What is ______ (*second character's*) point of view? How are they different?	How does the author use point of view to help the reader learn about the characters? Use the text to explain.	Use details from the text to show how the author uses different viewpoints to develop the characters.	How does the author use different viewpoints to enhance the development of the characters? Justify your response with evidence from the text.
How do ______ (*character's*) words/actions let us know his/her viewpoint? Use the text to explain.	How does the author show the point of view of ______ (*character*) over the course of the text? Use the text to explain.	How does the author develop ______ (*character's*) point of view through his/her speech and behavior? Use specific words and phrases from the text to support your answer.	How does the author develop ______ (*character's*) point of view without explicitly stating it in the text? Include text evidence in your response.
Does this text have a first- or third-person narrator? How do you know?	How would this text differ if it were told from the first-/third-person perspective? Explain.	Why does the author use first-/third-person perspective in this text? Support your answer with specific details from the text.	Is the narrator in this text omniscient? What language in the text gives you this information?

Identifying Point of View K–12 Alignment *(cont.)*

☆	○	□	△
How does ______ (*character's*) attitude affect the problem in the text?	Based on the events in the text, how does ______ (*character's*) attitude cause/create/affect the problem? Use details from the text in your answer.	How do the characters' opinions add to the conflict and its resolution? Explain your answer using examples from the text.	How do the characters' points of view contribute to the conflict and its resolution in the text? Justify your answer with text evidence.
How does the author/narrator feel about ______ (*character*)? How do you know?	What is the author's/narrator's point of view? What words let you know?	What is the author's/narrator's point of view? Use details from the text to support your answer.	What is the author's/narrator's viewpoint regarding ______ (*character*)? Provide evidence from the text to support your answer.
How is ______ (*character's*) viewpoint shown through conversation? Explain.	How is ______ (*character's*) viewpoint revealed through the conversations he/she has? Use the text to tell how you know.	How is ______ (*character's*) viewpoint expressed through the dialogue in the text? Use specific lines from the text to prove your answer.	How is ______ (*character's*) viewpoint expressed through the dialogue in the text? Include specific quotes from the text.
How does the author's/narrator's opinion affect how the events are told? Give an example.	How does the author's/narrator's point of view influence how the events are explained? Use the text to prove your answer.	How does the author's/narrator's point of view influence the description of the events that occur? Provide evidence from the text to support your answer.	How does the author's/narrator's viewpoint impact the description of the events that occur? Justify your answer with evidence from the text.
What culture does this text come from? How does that affect how the text is told?	What culture does this text come from? How does it affect the development of the text?	Explain how the culture this text comes from influences the way the text is told.	Explain how the culture this text comes from has an impact on the text. How would the text differ if it were told from a different cultural viewpoint?

Recognizing Figurative Language

Skill Overview

The most common forms of figurative language are simile, metaphor, personification, and hyperbole. They are used in everything from the picture books to college textbooks.

- A **simile** is a comparison that uses the words *like* or *as*. For example, "Lamar is as strong as an ox."
- A **metaphor** is a comparison that doesn't use *like* or *as*. For example, "She's climbing the ladder of success."
- **Personification** is giving human characteristics to an inanimate object. For example, "The trees danced in the wind."
- **Hyperbole** is gross exaggeration, often used to make a point or to promote humor. For example, "When are we going to eat? I'm starving!"

Use text-dependent questions to help your students to decipher figurative language and to discuss the importance of its use. Doing so will not only help their comprehension of text but also enhance their writing.

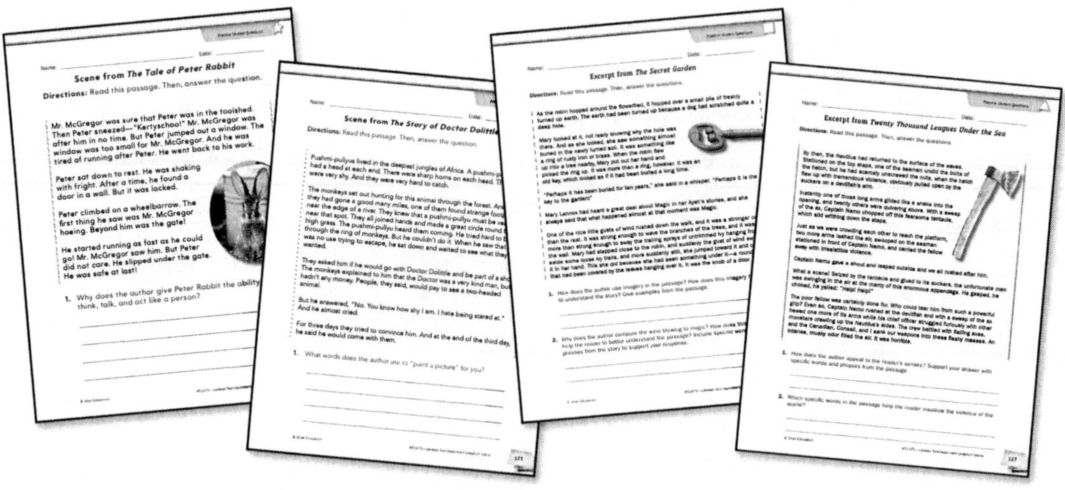

Implementing the Question Stems

This section includes 10 leveled, text-dependent question stems about recognizing figurative language. You can implement these question stems by connecting them to the fiction passages and/or nonfiction texts that you are reading in class.

It may seem as though using question stems would be easy, but it can be a complex task for teachers. To help you see how to implement these question stems in your classroom, this section includes student pages containing texts with sample text-dependent questions. Each of the four student pages illustrates a different complexity level.

Snapshot of Differentiating a Question

The chart below models how a single leveled question stem can be tied to both literature passages and informational texts at four complexity levels. This snapshot also gives you a quick view of how the question stems differ based on the complexity levels. However, you can also see how the question stems are linked to one another.

	Question Stem	Literature Example	Informational Text Example
☆	Why does the author use exaggeration? How does it help the text?	Why does the author use exaggeration in *The Five Chinese Brothers*? How does it help the story?	Why does the author use exaggeration? How does it help the text?
○	How does the author's use of simile/metaphor/personification/exaggeration help you to understand ______? Use the text to explain.	How does the author's use of exaggeration help you to understand *Matilda*? Use the book to explain.	How does the author's use of personification help you to understand the rain forest creatures? Use the text to explain.
□	How does the use of simile/metaphor/personification/hyperbole enhance your understanding of ______? Illustrate your answer with evidence from the text.	How does the use of hyperbole enhance your understanding of Pecos Bill? Illustrate your answer with evidence from the book.	How does the use of simile enhance your understanding of slavery? Illustrate your answer with evidence from the text.
△	How does the simile/metaphor/personification/hyperbole enhance the description of ______? Justify your response with textual evidence.	How does the hyperbole enhance the description in "The Celebrated Jumping Frog of Calaveras County"? Justify your response with textual evidence.	How does metaphor enhance the description in the essay? Justify your response with textual evidence.

COMPLEXITY

LOW

Recognizing Figurative Language Question Stems

Use these question stems to develop your own questions for students.

What words in the text help you to see ______ in your mind?

Which words help you to see/hear/smell ______?

How does the author "paint a picture" for you? Use words from the text to support your answer.

How does the author compare ______ to ______? What words are used?

Why does the author give ______ the ability to talk and act like a person?

Give an example of alliteration from the text.

Why does the author use exaggeration? How does it help the text?

Which words in the text are examples of onomatopoeia?

What words in the text tell about ______? How do they affect the way you see ______?

What can you tell about ______ from reading paragraph/page ______? Tell why.

Name: ______________________________ Date: ____________

Scene from *The Tale of Peter Rabbit*

Directions: Read this passage. Then, answer the question.

Mr. McGregor was sure that Peter was in the toolshed. Then Peter sneezed—"Kertyschoo!" Mr. McGregor was after him in no time. But Peter jumped out a window. The window was too small for Mr. McGregor. And he was tired of running after Peter. He went back to his work.

Peter sat down to rest. He was shaking with fright. After a time, he found a door in a wall. But it was locked.

Peter climbed on a wheelbarrow. The first thing he saw was Mr. McGregor hoeing. Beyond him was the gate!

He started running as fast as he could go! Mr. McGregor saw him. But Peter did not care. He slipped under the gate. He was safe at last!

1. Why does the author give Peter Rabbit the ability to think, talk, and act like a person?

____

____

____

____

COMPLEXITY

LOW    

Recognizing Figurative Language Question Stems

Use these question stems to develop your own questions for students.

Which words in the text help you to picture ______?

What words in the text tell about the sights/sounds/smells of ______?

What words does the author use to "paint a picture" for you?

Based on the events in the text, why does the author compare ______ to ______? What exact words are used?

Why does the author give ______ the ability to think, talk, and act like a person?

Offer an example of alliteration/simile/metaphor from the text. Why does the author play with language in this way?

How does the author's use of simile/metaphor/personification/exaggeration help you to understand ______? Use the text to explain.

How does the author use figurative language to tell about ______? Give examples from the text.

How does the figurative language used affect how you view ______? Use the text to explain.

What do you learn about ______ from the figurative language in the ______ paragraph? Use the text to explain.

Name: ______________________________ Date: ____________

Scene from *The Story of Doctor Dolittle*

Directions: Read this passage. Then, answer the question.

Pushmi-pullyus lived in the deepest jungles of Africa. A pushmi-pullyus had a head at each end. There were sharp horns on each head. They were very shy. And they were very hard to catch.

The monkeys set out hunting for this animal through the forest. And after they had gone a good many miles, one of them found strange footprints near the edge of a river. They knew that a pushmi-pullyu must be very near that spot. They all joined hands and made a great circle round the high grass. The pushmi-pullyu heard them coming. He tried hard to break through the ring of monkeys. But he couldn't do it. When he saw that it was no use trying to escape, he sat down and waited to see what they wanted.

They asked him if he would go with Doctor Dolittle and be part of a show. The monkeys explained to him that the Doctor was a very kind man, but hadn't any money. People, they said, would pay to see a two-headed animal.

But he answered, "No. You know how shy I am. I hate being stared at." And he almost cried.

For three days they tried to convince him. And at the end of the third day, he said he would come with them.

1. What words does the author use to "paint a picture" for you?

____

____

____

____

COMPLEXITY

LOW    

Recognizing Figurative Language Question Stems

Use these question stems to develop your own questions for students.

What are the exact words in the text that help the reader to envision ______?

How does the author help the reader to experience the sights/sounds/smells of ______? Quote words and phrases from the text.

How does the author use imagery in the text? How does this imagery help you to understand the text? Give examples from the text.

Why does the author compare ______ to ______? How does this comparison help the reader to better understand the text? Include specific words and phrases from the text to support your response.

What is the author's purpose in giving human characteristics to the ______?

Quote an example of alliteration/simile/metaphor from the text. What effect does this create?

How does the use of simile/metaphor/personification/hyperbole enhance your understanding of ______? Support your answer with evidence from the text.

Describe the kinds of figurative language the author uses in the text. Offer an example of each type using words from the text.

How does the author's use of figurative language affect the way the reader feels about ______? Offer examples from the text.

What does the author want the reader to infer from the figurative language in the ______ paragraph? Support your response with examples from the text.

Name: ______________________________ Date: ______________

Excerpt from *The Secret Garden*

Directions: Read this passage. Then, answer the questions.

As the robin hopped around the flowerbed, it hopped over a small pile of freshly turned up earth. The earth had been turned up because a dog had scratched quite a deep hole.

Mary looked at it, not really knowing why the hole was there. And as she looked, she saw something almost buried in the newly turned soil. It was something like a ring of rusty iron or brass. When the robin flew up into a tree nearby, Mary put out her hand and picked the ring up. It was more than a ring, however. It was an old key, which looked as if it had been buried a long time.

"Perhaps it has been buried for ten years," she said in a whisper. "Perhaps it is the key to the garden!"

Mary Lennox had heard a great deal about Magic in her Ayah's stories, and she always said that what happened almost at that moment was Magic.

One of the nice little gusts of wind rushed down the walk, and it was a stronger one than the rest. It was strong enough to wave the branches of the trees, and it was more than strong enough to sway the trailing sprays of untrimmed ivy hanging from the wall. Mary had stepped close to the robin, and suddenly the gust of wind swung aside some loose ivy trails, and more suddenly still, she jumped toward it and caught it in her hand. This she did because she had seen something under it—a round knob that had been covered by the leaves hanging over it. It was the knob of a door.

1. How does the author use imagery in the passage? How does this imagery help you to understand the story? Give examples from the passage.

____

____

2. Why does the author compare the wind blowing to magic? How does this comparison help the reader to better understand the passage? Include specific words and phrases from the story to support your response.

____

____

COMPLEXITY

LOW  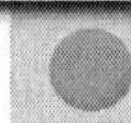  

Recognizing Figurative Language Question Stems

Use these question stems to develop your own questions for students.

Which specific words in the text help the reader visualize ______?

How does the author appeal to the reader's senses? Support your answer with specific words and phrases from the text.

What kind of imagery does the author use in the text, and how does it assist the reader in comprehending the text? Provide specific examples from the text.

What is the purpose of the comparison made between ______ and ______? How does it help the reader's comprehension? Use the text to illustrate your point.

What is the author's purpose in attributing human characteristics to an inanimate object such as ______?

Quote an example of alliteration/simile/metaphor from the text and describe its effect. Why does the author include this?

How does the simile/metaphor/personification/hyperbole enhance the description of ______? Justify your response with textual evidence.

Identify the types of figurative language the author uses. Provide specific examples from the text.

Use examples from the text to prove that the author uses figurative language to affect how the reader feels about ______.

What is the reader expected to infer from the figurative language in the ______ paragraph? Justify your answer with textual evidence.

Name: ______________________________ Date: ____________

Excerpt from *Twenty Thousand Leagues Under the Sea*

Directions: Read this passage. Then, answer the questions.

By then, the *Nautilus* had returned to the surface of the waves. Stationed on the top steps, one of the seamen undid the bolts of the hatch, but he had scarcely unscrewed the nuts, when the hatch flew up with tremendous violence, obviously pulled open by the suckers on a devilfish's arm.

Instantly one of those long arms glided like a snake into the opening, and twenty others were quivering above. With a sweep of the ax, Captain Nemo chopped off this fearsome tentacle, which slid writhing down the steps.

Just as we were crowding each other to reach the platform, two more arms lashed the air, swooped on the seaman stationed in front of Captain Nemo, and carried the fellow away with irresistible violence.

Captain Nemo gave a shout and leaped outside and we all rushed after him.

What a scene! Seized by the tentacle and glued to its suckers, the unfortunate man was swinging in the air at the mercy of this enormous appendage. He gasped, he choked, he yelled: "Help! Help!"

The poor fellow was certainly done for. Who could tear him from such a powerful grip? Even so, Captain Nemo rushed at the devilfish and with a sweep of the ax hewed one more of its arms while his chief officer struggled furiously with other monsters crawling up the *Nautilus's* sides. The crew battled with flailing axes, and the Canadian, Conseil, and I sank our weapons into these fleshy masses. An intense, musky odor filled the air. It was horrible.

1. How does the author appeal to the reader's senses? Support your answer with specific words and phrases from the passage.

   ____

   ____

2. Which specific words in the passage help the reader visualize the violence of the scene?

   ____

   ____

Recognizing Figurative Language K–12 Alignment

Use this chart to determine the best question stems for your different groups of students.

☆	○	□	△
What words in the text help you to see ______ in your mind?	Which words in the text help you to picture ______?	What are the exact words in the text that help the reader to envision ______?	Which specific words in the text help the reader visualize ______?
Which words help you to see/hear/smell ______?	What words in the text tell about the sights/sounds/smells of ______?	How does the author help the reader to experience the sights/sounds/smells of ______? Quote words and phrases from the text.	How does the author appeal to the reader's senses? Support your answer with specific words and phrases from the text.
How does the author "paint a picture" for you? Use words from the text to support your answer.	What words does the author use to "paint a picture" for you?	How does the author use imagery in the text? How does this imagery help you to understand the text? Give examples from the text.	What kind of imagery does the author use in the text, and how does it assist the reader in comprehending the text? Provide specific examples from the text.
How does the author compare ______ to ______? What words are used?	Based on the events in the text, why does the author compare ______ to ______? What exact words are used?	Why does the author compare ______ to ______? How does this comparison help the reader to better understand the text? Include specific words and phrases from the text to support your response.	What is the purpose of the comparison made between ______ and ______? How does it help the reader's comprehension? Use the text to illustrate your point.
Why does the author give ______ the ability to talk and act like a person?	Why does the author give ______ the ability to think, talk, and act like a person?	What is the author's purpose in giving human characteristics to the ______?	What is the author's purpose in attributing human characteristics to an inanimate object such as ______?

Recognizing Figurative Language K–12 Alignment *(cont.)*

☆	○	□	△
Give an example of alliteration from the text.	Offer an example of alliteration/simile/metaphor from the text. Why does the author play with language in this way?	Quote an example of alliteration/simile/metaphor from the text. What effect does this create?	Quote an example of alliteration/simile/metaphor from the text and describe its effect. Why does the author include this?
Why does the author use exaggeration? How does it help the text?	How does the author's use of simile/metaphor/personification/exaggeration help you to understand ______? Use the text to explain.	How does the use of simile/metaphor/personification/hyperbole enhance your understanding of ______? Support your answer with evidence from the text.	How does the simile/metaphor/personification/hyperbole enhance the description of ______? Justify your response with textual evidence.
Which words in the text are examples of onomatopoeia?	How does the author use figurative language to tell about ______? Give examples from the text.	Describe the kinds of figurative language the author uses in the text. Offer an example of each type using words from the text.	Identify the types of figurative language the author uses. Provide specific examples from the text.
What words in the text tell about ______? How do they affect the way you see ______?	How does the figurative language used affect how you view ______? Use the text to explain.	How does the author's use of figurative language affect the way the reader feels about ______? Offer examples from the text.	Use examples from the text to prove that the author uses figurative language to affect how the reader feels about ______.
What can you tell about ______ from reading paragraph/page ______? Tell why.	What do you learn about ______ from the figurative language in the ______ paragraph? Use the text to explain.	What does the author want the reader to infer from the figurative language in the ______ paragraph? Support your response with examples from the text.	What is the reader expected to infer from the figurative language in the ______ paragraph? Justify your answer with textual evidence.

Identifying Tone

Skill Overview

Tone is the author's attitude toward his or her written piece. Mood is the feeling that the piece invokes in the reader. Thus, the writer's tone can—and often does—affect the reader's mood.

The reader analyzes the tone to determine how to react to the piece. For example, if the tone is humorous, the reader realizes that author wants him or her to chuckle. If the tone is serious or angry, the reader understands that the author wants the reader to comprehend the gravity of the topic.

Tone can be a difficult literary element for students to grasp. As you read both fiction passages and nonfiction texts as a class, identify words or phrases that help to set the tone. Use a web graphic organizer to classify your ideas. Fill in the outer bubbles first with words that provide clues to the tone. Then, write the tone in the central circle. After you have done this twice as a class with different texts, have students fill out graphic organizers in smalls groups or in pairs for other texts they read.

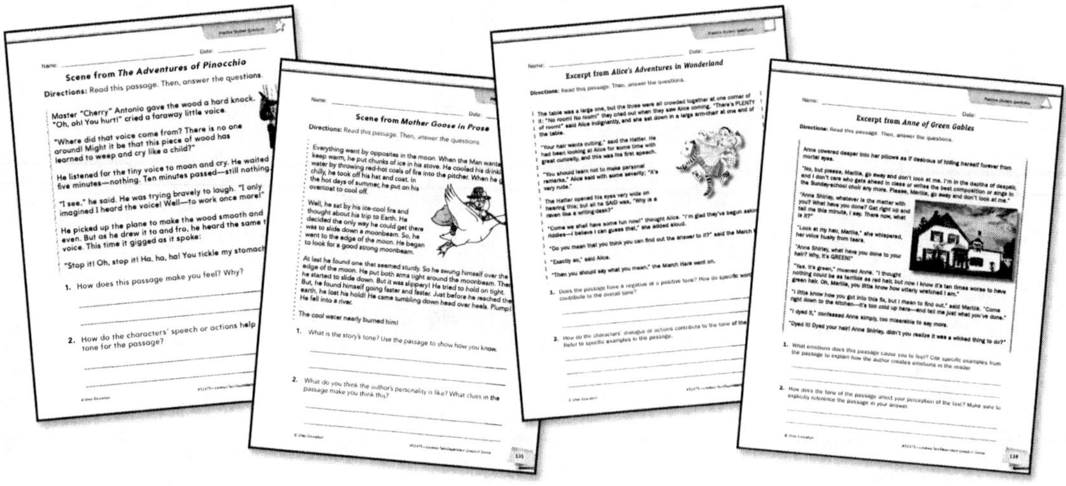
Scene from *The Adventures of Pinocchio*

Scene from *Mother Goose in Prose*

Excerpt from *Alice's Adventures in Wonderland*

Excerpt from *Anne of Green Gables*

Implementing the Question Stems

This section includes 10 leveled, text-dependent question stems about identifying tone. You can implement these question stems by connecting them to the fiction passages and/or nonfiction texts that you are reading in class.

It may seem as though using question stems would be easy, but it can be a complex task for teachers. To help you see how to implement these question stems in your classroom, this section includes student pages containing texts with sample text-dependent questions. Each of the four student pages illustrates a different complexity level.

Snapshot of Differentiating a Question

The chart below models how a single leveled question stem can be tied to both literature passages and informational texts at four complexity levels. This snapshot also gives you a quick view of how the question stems differ based on the complexity levels. However, you can also see how the question stems link to one another.

	Question Stem	Literature Example	Informational Text Example
☆	How does _____ (*character's*) speech/ actions add to the tone of the text? Give an example.	How do Biscuit's actions add to the tone of the story? Give an example.	How do Benjamin Franklin's actions add to the tone of the text? Give an example.
○	How does _____ (*character's*) conversation/behavior add to the tone of the text? Give specific text examples.	How does Mary's behavior add to the tone of the story in *The Secret Garden*? Give specific text examples.	How does Deborah Sampson's behavior add to the tone of the text? Give specific text examples.
□	How do the characters' dialogue or actions contribute to the tone of the text? Give specific text examples.	How does the dialogue between the settlers and the Mohawks contribute to the tone of the scene? Give specific text examples.	How does the Confederate soldiers' dialogue contribute to the tone of the text? Give specific text examples.
△	How do the characters' dialogue or actions contribute to the text's tone? Cite specific textual examples.	How does the characters' dialogue contribute to the novel's tone in *Of Mice and Men*? Cite specific textual examples.	How does the Representatives' dialogue contribute to the text's tone? Cite specific textual examples.

COMPLEXITY

LOW

Identifying Tone Question Stems

Use these question stems to develop your own questions for students.

How does this text make you feel? Why?

What is the tone of the text? What words let you know the tone?

Is the text's tone formal or casual? How do you know?

Does the text make you feel mad, glad, or sad? What words/ sentences help you to feel that way?

How does the text's tone make you feel about the text?

How do the characters' speech or actions help set the tone for the text?

How does the author feel about (*the subject matter/character*)? How do you know?

What is the author like? Why do you think so?

How does ______ (*character's*) speech or actions add to the tone of the text? Give an example.

Do you think that the author knows a lot about ______? Why? Give examples.

Name: ______________________________ Date: ____________

Scene from *The Adventures of Pinocchio*

Directions: Read this passage. Then, answer the questions.

Master "Cherry" Antonio gave the wood a hard knock. "Oh, oh! You hurt!" cried a faraway little voice.

"Where did that voice come from? There is no one around! Might it be that this piece of wood has learned to weep and cry like a child?"

He listened for the tiny voice to moan and cry. He waited five minutes—nothing. Ten minutes passed—still nothing.

"I see," he said. He was trying bravely to laugh. "I only imagined I heard the voice! Well—to work once more!"

He picked up the plane to make the wood smooth and even. But as he drew it to and fro, he heard the same tiny voice. This time it gigged as it spoke:

"Stop it! Oh, stop it! Ha, ha, ha! You tickle my stomach!"

1. How does this passage make you feel? Why?

____

____

2. How do the characters' speech or actions help set the tone for the passage?

____

____

COMPLEXITY

LOW    

Identifying Tone Question Stems

Use these question stems to develop your own questions for students.

How does this text make you feel? Tell what words the author uses to create this emotion.

What is the text's tone? Use the text to show how you know.

Does the author use a formal or a casual tone? What words or phrases let you know?

Is the text positive or negative? Use details to show how you know.

How does the text's tone affect your opinion of the text? Give examples from the text in your answer.

How do the characters' conversations or actions set the tone for the text? Give examples from the text.

How does the author feel about (*the subject matter/character*)? What words or phrases make this clear?

What do you think the author's personality is like? What clues in the text make you think this?

How does ______ (*character's*) conversations or behavior add to the tone of the text? Give specific text examples.

Does the author know a lot about ______? What information in the text makes you think so? Be specific.

Name: ______________________ Date: ____________

Scene from *Mother Goose in Prose*

Directions: Read this passage. Then, answer the questions.

Everything went by opposites in the moon. When the Man wanted to keep warm, he put chunks of ice in his stove. He cooled his drinking water by throwing red-hot coals of fire into the pitcher. When he got chilly, he took off his hat and coat. In the hot days of summer, he put on his overcoat to cool off.

Well, he sat by his ice-cool fire and thought about his trip to Earth. He decided the only way he could get there was to slide down a moonbeam. So, he went to the edge of the moon. He began to look for a good strong moonbeam.

At last he found one that seemed sturdy. So he swung himself over the edge of the moon. He put both arms tight around the moonbeam. Then he started to slide down. But it was slippery! He tried to hold on tight. But, he found himself going faster and faster. Just before he reached the earth, he lost his hold! He came tumbling down head over heels. Plump! He fell into a river.

The cool water nearly burned him!

1. What is the story's tone? Use the passage to show how you know.

____

____

2. What do you think the author's personality is like? What clues in the passage make you think this?

____

____

COMPLEXITY

LOW 

Identifying Tone Question Stems

Use these question stems to develop your own questions for students.

What emotions do you feel as you read the text? What words does the author use to create this emotion? Use specific examples from the text.

What words and phrases does the author use to create the tone? Give examples from the text.

Does the text have a formal or a casual tone? State specific words or phrases that contribute to the tone.

Does the text have a negative or a positive tone? How do specific words choices contribute to the overall tone?

How does the tone of the text affect your perception of the text? Refer to specific examples from the text in your answer.

How do the characters' dialogue or actions contribute to the tone of the text? Refer to specific examples in the text.

What is the author's opinion of (*the subject matter/character*)? What specific words in the text make you think this?

What do you imagine the author's personality is like? How is his/her personality expressed through the text? Use examples from the text to explain your thinking.

How do the characters' dialogue or actions contribute to the tone of the text? Give specific text examples.

Is the author an expert in ______? What specific information in the text makes you believe this?

Name: ______________________ Date: ____________

Excerpt from *Alice's Adventures in Wonderland*

Directions: Read this passage. Then, answer the questions.

The table was a large one, but the three were all crowded together at one corner of it: "No room! No room!" they cried out when they saw Alice coming. "There's PLENTY of room!" said Alice indignantly, and she sat down in a large arm-chair at one end of the table.

"Your hair wants cutting," said the Hatter. He had been looking at Alice for some time with great curiosity, and this was his first speech.

"You should learn not to make personal remarks," Alice said with some severity; "it's very rude."

The Hatter opened his eyes very wide on hearing this; but all he SAID was, "Why is a raven like a writing-desk?"

"Come we shall have some fun now!" thought Alice. "I'm glad they've begun asking riddles—I believe I can guess that," she added aloud.

"Do you mean that you think you can find out the answer to it?" said the March Hare.

"Exactly so," said Alice.

"Then you should say what you mean," the March Hare went on.

1. Does the passage have a negative or a positive tone? How do specific words choices contribute to the overall tone?

____

____

2. How do the characters' dialogue or actions contribute to the tone of the story? Refer to specific examples in the passage.

____

____

____

Identifying Tone Question Stems

Use these question stems to develop your own questions for students.

- What emotions does this text cause you to feel? Cite specific examples from the text to explain how the author creates emotions in the reader.
- What language does the author use to create the tone? Cite specific examples from the text.
- Does the author use a formal or casual tone? Identify specific words or phrases that contribute to the tone.
- Does the text have a negative or a positive tone? Identify specific words that contribute to the overall tone.
- How does the tone of the text affect your perception of the text? Make sure to explicitly reference the text in your answer.
- How do the characters' dialogue or behaviors contribute to the tone of the text? Cite textual examples of dialogue/behaviors in your answer.
- What is the author's opinion of (*the subject matter/character*)? What clues in the text language convey the author's attitude?
- What do you imagine the author's personality is like? How is his/her personality expressed through the language of the text? Use specific textual examples to support your response.
- How do the characters' dialogue or actions contribute to the text's tone? Cite specific textual examples.
- Is the author an expert in ______? Give textual examples to illustrate your opinion.

Name: ______________________ Date: __________

Excerpt from *Anne of Green Gables*

Directions: Read this passage. Then, answer the questions.

Anne cowered deeper into her pillows as if desirous of hiding herself forever from mortal eyes.

"No, but please, Marilla, go away and don't look at me. I'm in the depths of despair, and I don't care who gets ahead in class or writes the best composition or sings in the Sunday-school choir any more. Please, Marilla, go away and don't look at me."

"Anne Shirley, whatever is the matter with you? What have you done? Get right up and tell me this minute, I say. There now, what is it?"

"Look at my hair, Marilla," she whispered, her voice husky from tears.

"Anne Shirley, what have you done to your hair? Why, it's GREEN!"

"Yes, it's green," moaned Anne. "I thought nothing could be as terrible as red hair, but now I know it's ten times worse to have green hair. Oh, Marilla, you little know how utterly wretched I am."

"I little know how you got into this fix, but I mean to find out," said Marilla. "Come right down to the kitchen—it's too cold up here—and tell me just what you've done."

"I dyed it," confessed Anne simply, too miserable to say more.

"Dyed it! Dyed your hair! Anne Shirley, didn't you realize it was a wicked thing to do?"

1. What emotions does this passage cause you to feel? Cite specific examples from the passage to explain how the author creates emotions in the reader.

____

____

2. How does the tone of the passage affect your perception of the text? Make sure to explicitly reference the passage in your answer.

____

____

Identifying Tone K–12 Alignment

Use this chart to determine the best question stems for your different groups of students.

☆	○	□	△
How does this text make you feel? Why?	How does this text make you feel? Tell what words the author uses to create this emotion.	What emotions do you feel as you read the text? What words does the author use to create this emotion? Use specific examples from the text.	What emotions does this text cause you to feel? Cite specific examples from the text to explain how the author creates emotions in the reader.
What is the tone of the text? What words let you know the tone?	What is the text's tone? Use the text to show how you know.	What words and phrases does the author use to create the tone? Give examples from the text.	What language does the author use to create the tone? Cite specific examples from the text.
Is the text's tone formal or casual? How do you know?	Does the author use a formal or a casual tone? What words or phrases let you know?	Does the text have a formal or a casual tone? State specific words or phrases that contribute to the tone.	Does the author use a formal or casual tone? Identify specific words or phrases that contribute to the tone.
Does the text make you feel mad, glad or sad? What words/sentences help you to feel that way?	Is the text positive or negative? Use details to show how you know.	Does the text have a negative or a positive tone? How do specific words choices contribute to the overall tone?	Does the text have a negative or a positive tone? Identify specific words that contribute to the overall tone.
How does the text's tone make you feel about the text?	How does the text's tone affect your opinion of the text? Give examples from the text in your answer.	How does the tone of the text affect your perception of the text? Refer to specific examples from the text in your answer.	How does the tone of the text affect your perception of the text? Make sure to explicitly reference the text in your answer.

Identifying Tone K–12 Alignment *(cont.)*

☆	○	□	△
How do the characters' speech or actions help set the tone for the text?	How do the characters' conversations or actions set the tone for the text? Give examples from the text.	How do the characters' dialogue or actions contribute to the tone of the text? Refer to specific examples in the text.	How do the characters' dialogue or behaviors contribute to the tone of the text? Cite textual examples of dialogue/behaviors in your answer.
How does the author feel about (*the subject matter/character*)? How do you know?	How does the author feel about (*the subject matter/character*)? What words or phrases make this clear?	What is the author's opinion of (*the subject matter/character*)? What specific words in the text make you think this?	What is the author's opinion of (*the subject matter/character*)? What clues in the text language convey the author's attitude?
What is the author like? Why do you think so?	What do you think the author's personality is like? What clues in the text make you think this?	What do you imagine the author's personality is like? How is his/her personality expressed through the text? Use examples from the text to explain your thinking.	What do you imagine the author's personality is like? How is his/her personality expressed through the language of the text? Use specific textual examples to support your response.
How does ______ (*character's*) speech or actions add to the tone of the text? Give an example.	How does ______ (*character's*) conversations or behavior add to the tone of the text? Give specific text examples.	How do the characters' dialogue or actions contribute to the tone of the text? Give specific text examples.	How do the characters' dialogue or actions contribute to the text's tone? Cite specific textual examples.
Do you think that the author knows a lot about ______? Why? Give examples.	Does the author know a lot about ______? What information in the text makes you think so? Be specific.	Is the author an expert in ______? What specific information in the text makes you believe this?	Is the author an expert in ______? Give textual examples to illustrate your opinion.

Making Inferences

Skill Overview

By definition, inferences are not explicitly stated in the text. Instead, the reader must ascertain the implicit connection between pieces of information to understand the text. Often students do not even realize that they may have misunderstood or completely missed an inference in the text. They may keep reading without ever gaining a full understanding of what is implied. This missed opportunity often affects overall comprehension of the text.

Inference-based, text-dependent questions can call students' attention to inferences, and highlight the structure of the language that makes the inferences possible and necessary. In this way, text-dependent questions help students to notice that an inference is necessary, to explain it, and to examine the purpose behind the author's use of the inference in the text.

As students become more proficient, text-dependent questions can move away from directing students to a specific use of an inference and allow them to select their own text-based evidence for support.

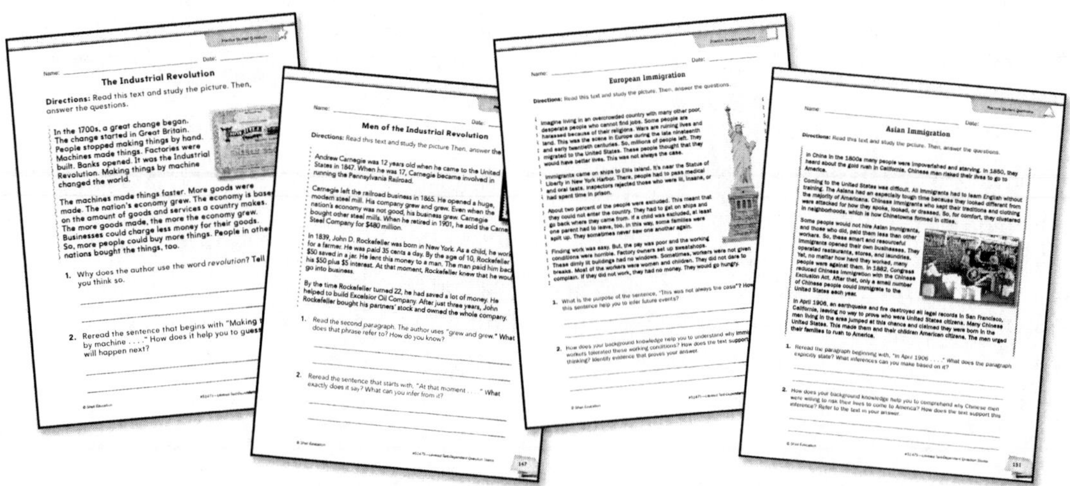

Implementing the Question Stems

This section includes 10 leveled, text-dependent question stems about making inferences. You can implement these question stems by connecting them to the fiction passages and/or nonfiction texts that you are reading in class.

It may seem as though using question stems would be easy, but it can be a complex task for teachers. To help you see how to implement these question stems in your classroom, this section includes student pages containing texts with sample text-dependent questions. Each of the four student pages illustrates a different complexity level.

Snapshot of Differentiating a Question

The chart below models how a single leveled question stem can be tied to both literature passages and informational texts at four complexity levels. This snapshot also gives you a quick view of how the question stems differ based on the complexity levels. However, you can also see how the question stems link to one another.

	Question Stem	Literature Example	Informational Text Example
☆	Why does ______ (*character*) feel ______? What words in the text let you know?	Why does Buzz feel surprised? What words in the book let you know?	Why does George Washington feel like he should fight in the war? What words in the text let you know?
○	Why does ______ (*character*) feel ______? State the words or phrases from the text that make you think so.	Why does Caleb feel sad when Sarah leaves? State the words or phrases from the book that make you think so.	Why does the scientist feel that the boat would float better in salt water? State the words or phrases from the text that make you think so.
□	Why does ______ (*character*) feel ______? Include the specific words or phrases from the text in your answer.	Why does Stanley feel so close to Zero? Include the specific words or phrases from the novel in your answer.	Why does Abraham Lincoln feel that McClellan is not the right leader for the Union Army? Include the specific words or phrases from the text in your answer.
△	Why does ______ (*character*) feel ______ in paragraph on page ______? Include specific words or phrases from the text in your response.	Why does Nick feel jealous of Gatsby in the fourth paragraph on page 98? Include specific words or phrases from the text in your response.	Why does Napoleon feel angry in the description on page 128? Include specific words or phrases from the text in your response.

COMPLEXITY

LOW  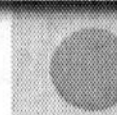  

Making Inferences Question Stems

Use these question stems to develop your own questions for students.

What can you tell about _____? How do you know?

Why does the author use the word ". . ."? Tell why you think so.

The author writes ". . . ." Why? How do you know?

What do you think will happen to _____ (*character*) by the end of the paragraph/chapter? Why?

What do you already know about _____? What words in the text tell you more about it?

Reread the sentence that begins with ". . . ." How does it help you to guess what will happen next?

What does the narrator feel/think? What words let you know?

Reread the sentence/paragraph that starts with ". . . ." What does it say? What does it let you know about _____?

Why does _____ (*character*) feel _____? What words in the text let you know?

Think about _____ (*character's*) conversation with _____ (*character*). What do you think will happen based on their talk?

Name: ______________________________ Date: ______________

The Industrial Revolution

Directions: Read this text and study the picture. Then, answer the questions.

In the 1700s, a great change began. The change started in Great Britain. People stopped making things by hand. Machines made things. Factories were built. Banks opened. It was the Industrial Revolution. Making things by machine changed the world.

The machines made things faster. More goods were made. The nation's economy grew. The economy is based on the amount of goods and services a country makes. The more goods made, the more the economy grew. Businesses could charge less money for their goods. So, more people could buy more things. People in other nations bought the things, too.

1. Why does the author use the word *revolution*? Tell why you think so.

____

____

2. Reread the sentence that begins with "Making things by machine . . . ." How does it help you to guess what will happen next?

____

____

COMPLEXITY

LOW

Making Inferences Question Stems

Use these question stems to develop your own questions for students.

Reread the ______ sentence/paragraph. What does the author mean? Use the text to tell how you know.

Read the ______ sentence. The author uses ". . . ." What does that word refer to? How do you know?

The author writes ". . ." in the ______ paragraph. Why? What do you already know that helped to figure it out?

What can you infer will happen by the end of the ______ paragraph/chapter? Why do you think so?

How can you use what you already know to understand ______? What words in the text support your thinking?

Why does the author write ". . ."? How does it help you to predict what will happen next?

What does the narrator feel/think about ______? Use the text to tell how you know.

Reread the sentence/paragraph that starts with ". . . ." What exactly does it say? What can you infer from it?

Why does ______ (*character*) feel ______? State the words or phrases from the text that make you think so.

What can you tell from the conversation on page/paragraph ______? Give evidence from the text as support.

Name: ______________________ Date: ____________

Men of the Industrial Revolution

Directions: Read this text and study the picture Then, answer the questions.

Andrew Carnegie was 12 years old when he came to the United States in 1847. When he was 17, Carnegie became involved in running the Pennsylvania Railroad.

Carnegie left the railroad business in 1865. He opened a huge, modern steel mill. His company grew and grew. Even when the nation's economy was not good, his business grew. Carnegie bought other steel mills. When he retired in 1901, he sold the Carnegie Steel Company for $480 million.

In 1839, John D. Rockefeller was born in New York. As a child, he worked for a farmer. He was paid 35 cents a day. By the age of 10, Rockefeller had $50 saved in a jar. He lent this money to a man. The man paid him back his $50 plus $5 interest. At that moment, Rockefeller knew that he would go into business.

By the time Rockefeller turned 22, he had saved a lot of money. He helped to build Excelsior Oil Company. After just three years, John Rockefeller bought his partners' stock and owned the whole company.

1. Read the second paragraph. The author uses "grew and grew." What does that phrase refer to? How do you know?

____

____

2. Reread the sentence that starts with, "At that moment . . . ." What exactly does it say? What can you infer from it?

____

____

COMPLEXITY

LOW  

Making Inferences Question Stems

Use these question stems to develop your own questions for students.

What does the author want you to infer from the ______ sentence/paragraph? Use text evidence to support your answer.

In the ______ sentence/paragraph, the author uses the word ". . . ." To what does the word refer? Use the text to explain how you know.

The author writes ". . ." in the ______ paragraph. Why? What background knowledge do you use to figure it out?

What can you infer will occur by the end of the ______ paragraph/chapter? How do you know?

How does your background knowledge help you to understand ______? How does the text support your thinking? Identify evidence that proves your answer.

What is the purpose of the sentence ". . ."? How does this sentence help you to infer future events?

How does the narrator feel/think about ______? How do you know? Use text evidence to support your answer.

Reread the sentence/paragraph that starts with ". . . ." What exactly does the sentence/paragraph say? What does it imply?

Why does ______ (*character*) feel ______? Include specific words or phrases from the text in your answer.

What can you infer from the dialogue on page ______? State evidence from the text to support your ideas.

Name: ______________________ Date: ____________

European Immigration

Directions: Read this text and study the picture. Then, answer the questions.

Imagine living in an overcrowded country with many other poor, desperate people who cannot find jobs. Some people are harassed because of their religions. Wars are ruining lives and land. This was the scene in Europe during the late nineteenth and early twentieth centuries. So, millions of people left. They migrated to the United States. These people thought that they would have better lives. This was not always the case.

Immigrants came on ships to Ellis Island. It's near the Statue of Liberty in New York Harbor. There, people had to pass medical and oral tests. Inspectors rejected those who were ill, insane, or had spent time in prison.

About two percent of the people were excluded. This meant that they could not enter the country. They had to get on ships and go back where they came from. If a child was excluded, at least one parent had to leave, too. In this way, some families were split up. They sometimes never saw one another again.

Finding work was easy. But, the pay was poor and the working conditions were horrible. Factory owners set up sweatshops. These dimly lit buildings had no windows. Sometimes, workers were not given breaks. Most of the workers were women and children. They did not dare to complain. If they did not work, they had no money. They would go hungry.

1. What is the purpose of the sentence, "This was not always the case"? How does this sentence help you to infer future events?

____

____

2. How does your background knowledge help you to understand why immigrant workers tolerated these working conditions? How does the text support your thinking? Identify evidence that proves your answer.

____

____

COMPLEXITY

LOW 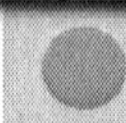  

Making Inferences Question Stems

Use these question stems to develop your own questions for students.

What inference does the author want you to make from the _____ sentence/paragraph? Support your answer with textual evidence.

In the _____ sentence/paragraph, the author writes the word ". . . ." Use evidence from the text to explain what the word refers to.

In the _____ paragraph, the author writes ". . . ." What does this mean? What prior knowledge do you use to make this inference?

What inference can you make about what will occur by the end of the _____ paragraph/chapter? Explain how the text helps you to draw this conclusion.

How does your background knowledge help you to comprehend _____? How does the text support this inference? Refer to the text in your answer.

What is the purpose of the sentence ". . ."? How does this sentence help you make inferences about future events?

How does the narrator feel/believe/think about _____ in the passage? Include textual evidence to support your answer.

Reread the sentence/paragraph beginning with ". . . ." What does the sentence/paragraph explicitly state? What inferences can you make based on it?

Why does _____ (*character*) feel _____ in paragraph/on page _____? Include specific words or phrases from the text in your response.

What inferences can you make from the dialogue on page/paragraph _____? What evidence from the text supports these inferences?

Name: ______________________________ Date: ______________

Asian Immigration

Directions: Read this text and study the picture. Then, answer the questions.

In China in the 1800s many people were impoverished and starving. In 1850, they heard about the gold rush in California. Chinese men risked their lives to go to America.

Coming to the United States was difficult. All immigrants had to learn English without training. The Asians had an especially tough time because they looked different from the majority of Americans. Chinese immigrants who kept their traditions and clothing were attacked for how they spoke, looked, or dressed. So, for comfort, they clustered in neighborhoods, which is how Chinatowns formed in cities.

Some people would not hire Asian immigrants, and those who did, paid them less than other workers. So, these smart and resourceful immigrants opened their own businesses. They operated restaurants, stores, and laundries. Yet, no matter how hard they worked, many people were against them. In 1882, Congress reduced Chinese immigration with the Chinese Exclusion Act. After that, only a small number of Chinese people could immigrate to the United States each year.

In April 1906, an earthquake and fire destroyed all legal records in San Francisco, California, leaving no way to prove who were United States citizens. Many Chinese men living in the area jumped at this chance and claimed they were born in the United States. This made them and their children American citizens. The men urged their families to rush to America.

1. Reread the paragraph beginning with, "In April 1906 . . . ." What does the paragraph explicitly state? What inferences can you make based on it?

____

____

2. How does your background knowledge help you to comprehend why Chinese men were willing to risk their lives to come to America? How does the text support this inference? Refer to the text in your answer.

____

____

Making Inferences K–12 Alignment

Use this chart to determine the best question stems for your different groups of students.

☆	○	□	△
What can you tell about ______? How do you know?	Reread the ______ sentence/paragraph. What does the author mean? Use the text to tell how you know.	What does the author want you to infer from the ______ sentence/ paragraph? Use text evidence to support your answer.	What inference does the author want you to make from the ______ sentence/ paragraph? Support your answer with textual evidence.
Why does the author use the word ". . ."? Tell why you think so.	Read the ______ sentence. The author uses ". . . ." What does that word refer to? How do you know?	In the ______ sentence/paragraph, the author uses the word ". . . ." To what does the word refer? Use the text to explain how you know.	In the ______ sentence/paragraph, the author writes the word ". . . ." Use evidence from the text to explain what the word refers to.
The author writes ". . . ." Why? How do you know?	The author writes ". . ." in the ______ paragraph. Why? What do you already know that helped to figure it out?	The author writes ". . ." in the ______ paragraph. Why? What background knowledge do you use to figure it out?	In the ______ paragraph, the author writes ". . . ." What does this mean? What prior knowledge do you use to make this inference?
What do you think will happen to ______ (*character*) by the end of the paragraph/ chapter? Why?	What can you infer will happen by the end of the ______ paragraph/ chapter? Why do you think so?	What can you infer will occur by the end of the ______ paragraph/ chapter? How do you know?	What inference can you make about what will occur by the end of the ______ paragraph/chapter? Explain how the text helps you to draw this conclusion.
What do you already know about ______? What words in the text tell you more about it?	How can you use what you already know to understand ______? What words in the text support your thinking?	How does your background knowledge help you to understand ______? How does the text support your thinking? Identify evidence that proves your answer.	How does your background knowledge help you to comprehend ______? How does the text support this inference? Refer to the text in your answer.

Making Inferences K–12 Alignment *(cont.)*

☆	○	□	△
Reread the sentence that begins with ". . . ." How does it help you to guess what will happen next?	Why does the author write ". . ."? How does it help you to predict what will happen next?	What is the purpose of the sentence ". . ."? How does this sentence help you to infer future events?	What is the purpose of the sentence ". . ."? How does this sentence help you make inferences about future events?
What does the narrator feel/think? What words let you know?	What does the narrator feel/think about ______? Use the text to tell how you know.	How does the narrator feel/think about ______? How do you know? Use text evidence to support your answer.	How does the narrator feel/believe/think about ______ in the passage? Include textual evidence to support your answer.
Reread the sentence/paragraph that starts with ". . . ." What does it say? What does it let you know about ______?	Reread the sentence/paragraph that starts with ". . . ." What exactly does it say? What can you infer from it?	Reread the sentence/paragraph that starts with ". . . ." What exactly does the sentence/paragraph say? What does it imply?	Reread the sentence/paragraph beginning with ". . . ." What does the sentence/paragraph explicitly state? What inferences can you make based on it?
Why does ______ (*character*) feel ______? What words in the text let you know?	Why does ______ (*character*) feel ______? State the words or phrases from the text that make you think so.	Why does ______ (*character*) feel ______? Include specific words or phrases from the text in your answer.	Why does ______ (*character*) feel ______ in paragraph/on page ______? Include specific words or phrases from the text in your response.
Think about ______ (*character's*) conversation with ______ (*character*). What do you think will happen based on their talk?	What can you tell from the conversation on page/paragraph ______? Give evidence from the text as support.	What can you infer from the dialogue on page ______? State evidence from the text to support your ideas.	What inferences can you make from the dialogue on page/paragraph ______? What evidence from the text supports these inferences?

Answer Key

Different Atoms, Different Things (page 13)

1. The main idea of the text is that atoms make up all the different things in the world. The main idea comes from the first paragraph.
2. The text explains oxygen atoms as ones that "grab other atoms" all the time.

Atoms, Elements, Molecules, and Compounds (page 15)

1. A compound is described as molecules with "different types of atoms."
2. The purpose of this text is to inform readers. We can learn about atoms, elements, molecules, and compounds by reading this text.

States of Matter (page 17)

1. The states of matter are introduced through examples of water as solid ice that "you can skate on," a liquid "you can swim in," and as a vapor "as steam from a kettle."
2. The lesson of this text is to inform readers about the various states of matter using water molecules as the primary example.

The Periodic Table (page 19)

1. The author introduces changes in the Periodic Table by stating that Mendeleév "believed that elements would be found to fill" gaps that occurred in the table.
2. The purpose of this text is to inform readers. We learn about the history of the periodic table and how it is organized.

Fugitive Slave Act (page 25)

1. Any of the following terms are examples of words that tell about slavery: free state, sued, United States Supreme Court, property, rights, and freedom.
2. The text states that Dred Scott was a slave whose owner moved from a slave state to a free state and a free territory. That is why Dred Scott and others thought he should be free. However, the U.S. Supreme Court decided he was property and could not be free.

The Civil War Begins (page 27)

1. The main idea is that the Civil War was the worst war in United States history. More Americans died during this war than in any other war. Facts that support this main idea: Fort Sumter went up in flames; the Union Army had 34,000 soldiers at the Battle of Bull Run, but the Confederates still sent the Union soldiers running; the painting also supports the main idea.
2. The author puts the supporting details in this order because they are in the order of what happened in the Civil War.

The Civil War Ends (page 29)

1. The main idea of this paragraph is that despite huge Union victories, the war continued on for a long time. Supporting details include: "Northerners hoped that the war would end quickly, but it was another two years before the fighting ceased." ". . . the two armies fought from June 1864 until the next April."
2. The main people are General Lee of the Confederacy and General Grant of the Union. From this passage, there are several important details that can influence your students' opinions about them. Be sure that your students provide some of these details to support their opinions.

   General Lee lost at Gettysburg. Despite the loss, General Lee continued leading the Confederate army for two more years. Lee had lost too many men, so he withdrew from Petersburg on April 2, 1865. He surrendered soon after at Appomattox Court House.

   It was General Grant's job to capture Vicksburg. He laid siege to Vicksburg. This forced the rebels to surrender, giving Grant a victory. Grant accepted Lee's surrender.

Civil War Leaders (page 31)

1. Lincoln wanted to keep the country united. In early 1864, Ulysses S. Grant was named the commander of the Union Army. Lincoln needed to win the war.

Answer Key *(cont.)*

2. The order in which the details are presented, though not in chronological order, show that each of the different leaders of the Civil War played important roles, no matter if they were the president of the country or the general of an army.

Ancient Greece (page 37)

1. Each student's response will vary, however all responses should include: The Greeks built temples for the gods. The Greeks wrote plays held in the city-state of Athens. The Greeks came up with various treatments for the ill.
2. The main events of the text include Athens holding the first public plays and the Greeks solving medical issues.

Greek City-States (page 39)

1. The city-states of Athens and Sparta, though both Greek, had very different cultures. People of Athens valued intellectual and artistic strength and beauty, while the people of Sparta valued their army and having a strong Spartan pride.
2. The key details of this paragraph include: Sparta was known for its brave troops. Every male belonged to Sparta and had to serve in the army. Spartans believed working hard, doing your duty, and dying for Sparta was an honorable way to live.

The Beautiful City of Rome (page 41)

1. Two brothers, Romulus and Remus, were raised by a wolf, built part of a city, and fought. Romulus murdered his brother, became king, and named the city Rome. The Roman people built arches and columns much like that of ancient Greece, but were the first to put domes on buildings. For many years, Rome was ruled by kings, but later became the Roman Republic, which lasted for almost 500 years.

   The sequence of events here is important and it shows the growth and strength of the city of Rome.
2. The central idea of the text is the history of the early years of Rome. Key details include the two brothers Romulus and Remus, the Romans' beautiful architecture, and the Roman Republic.

The Rise and Fall of the Roman Empire (page 43)

1. The Roman Empire had legionnaires who helped Rome fight to win more land. To help with expensive military equipment, Roman people paid taxes to help cover the costs. The Roman Empire grew so large that it became more vulnerable to an attack, causing the Roman Empire to collapse and split into two halves—the Easter Empire and the Western Empire. Even though the Roman Empire collapsed, people and cultures today are still influenced by the ancient Romans.
2. The main event in this passage is the fall of the Roman Empire in A.D. 476. This fall was due to the empire's "large size" and "long border" that made it "vulnerable to attack" and easy for enemies to "weaken the borders."

Understanding Place Value to 6 Digits (page 49)

1. The chart in the text shows how place values work.

Special Kinds of Numbers (page 51)

1. The author includes the chart to more easily show how various integers are grouped together. It allows for a simpler and more visual understanding of even and odd integers, as well as prime and composite numbers.
2. The bold words are set apart from the rest to indicate that readers should pay special attention to those particular sentences or the ones following, as they explain and give brief definitions of the bolded words.

Understanding the Language of Factors and Multiples (page 53)

1. The reader can quickly search for information in this text by looking for the bold font. The reader may also look for numbers in each definition, as they provide mathematical examples, such as 5 x 7 = 35.
2. The author uses bold font to indicate to the reader each new subject or concept.

Answer Key *(cont.)*

Comparing and Ordering Whole Numbers (page 55)

1. The chart provides a four-step solution to finding the order in which a set of numbers is either ascending or descending. The steps include lining up the numbers by place value, comparing the digits beginning with the greatest placeholder, and continuing to the right until a difference in the numbers is found.
2. The words "ascending order" and "descending order" are printed in bold to provide readers with an indication that these are the two main concepts that this section will be focusing on. The bold font provides an easy way for readers to locate definitions and examples of the concepts.

Scene from *Robinson Crusoe* (page 61)

1. The setting is in the ocean in a storm.
2. On one hand, it would completely change the scene (i.e., if it were not stormy). On the other hand, it might not change it at all (it doesn't matter if this happened yesterday or 50 years ago. If a person is washed ashore during a storm onto a deserted island, the scene/setting would be the same).

Scene from *The Wonderful Wizard of Oz* (page 63)

1. The entire City is green. The buildings are made of green marble and covered in emeralds. The pavement, windowpanes, and sky are green. The people are dressed in green and even have greenish skin. There's "green candy and green popcorn . . .green shoes, green hats, and green clothes of all sorts."
2. Having an all-green setting helps to shape the overall tone of this scene as it enhances the feeling of being somewhere new. The tone here has a sense of wonderment, confusion, and intrigue. Reading about the details of the green city not only allows readers to imagine what the city looks like but to experience it with Dorothy as well.

Excerpt from *The Hound of the Baskervilles* (page 65)

1. The setting is the road leading up to the "maze of fantastic tracery in wrought iron" that is the home of the Baskervilles.
2. Traveling by "stunted oaks and firs that had been twisted and bent by the fury of the storms" and passing through a "somber tunnel" at the Baskerville house that is "marked by the boars' heads" enhance the ominous tone of the text.

Excerpt from *The Adventures of Tom Sawyer* (page 67)

1. The setting of the church makes Tom bored and means he will find a means of entertainment in any way he can.
2. The author states that the "the minister droned monotonously through a sermon so boring that many a-head began to nod" to indicate the depressing setting is inside the church.

Working It Out (page 73)

1. Students will give varying answers about how the fight makes them feel including: upset, annoyed, angry, or frustrated. Words or phrases used in the passage to create such emotions might include "No!" "That is too bad," or "I am telling Mom!"
2. The turning point in the scene is when Mom says to Grace, "You know, Grace, you two are a lot alike." This enables Grace to realize that Nina and she argue because they care about each other a lot and have a lot in common with one another.

Eunice's Family (page 75)

1. Eunice's parents assure her that "a real family is made up of people who love each other" and this shows that Eunice is loved and is an important member of the family no matter what.

Excerpt from *Much Ado About Nothing* (page 77)

1. Playing a trick on Benedick is the main event that sets up a potential conflict for the remainder of the play. It also allows for a glimpse into the personalities of each of the characters.

Answer Key *(cont.)*

2. As the script progresses, we begin to see more of the mean-spirited characteristics of Claudio and Don Pedro. The further their trick goes, the more pleasure the two take in the fact that Benedick "believes what [they] are saying about Beatrice."

Excerpt from *Macbeth* (page 79)

1. The climax of this scene is when Macbeth says to himself, "Part of me feels such extreme guilt for what I am considering doing to him, but another part of me craves the power he has and wants to do whatever is needed to have it." This moment shows Macbeth's internal struggle that will later be resolved when he states that he no longer wishes to go through with the plan.
2. This line shows that Lady Macbeth holds most of the power in the relationship between her and her husband. By reminding Macbeth that he should be hiding in Duncan's room, Lady Macbeth is taking charge of her husband and attempting to remind him of his duty. This also inadvertently shows that she is the one who cares most about gaining power.

Scene from *The Prince and the Pauper* (page 85)

1. Though no words are used to directly tell about Tom, "Tom's breath came quick" and "cut short with excitement" tell that he is anxious and excited to see the young prince.
2. The prince says this to stand up for Tom the pauper. This suggests that the prince has a kind heart and does not want to see anyone, no matter what their stature, harmed or mistreated.

Scene from *A Little Princess* (page 87)

1. Through this passage it is evident that Sara does not hold much confidence in herself. She feels that she is ugly even though others see her as a beautiful young girl.
2. Sara feels that Miss Minchin "is telling a story" by saying Sara is a beautiful child. Sara seems very untrusting of Miss Minchin, and is "not at all pleased by Miss Minchin's flattery."

Excerpt from *Rainbow Valley* (page 89)

1. Mary is upset and troubled. She doesn't reply when asked a question and instead sits suddenly on the hay and cries.
2. Faith is a caring person who is willing to do whatever she can for her friends. The author communicates this by telling that "Faith had flung herself down beside her," and commanding to Mary, "You come right up to the manse and get something to eat before you say another word."

Excerpt from *Little Women* (page 91)

1. Jo is adventurous and slightly mischievous. She enjoys doing "Daring things" and is "always scandalizing." She is interested in learning more about the Laurence boy, and helping him in attaining more "society and fun."
2. Jo's motivation stems from her disdain for Mr. Laurence's attempt to keep the Laurence boy "shut up all alone."

Every Family Has a History (page 97)

1. The setting is not directly stated, but it is likely taking place in a living room since the text describes Marcus as sitting on a sofa. The three main characters are Nora, Marcus, and Meme.

Booker T. Washington (page 99)

1. This passage is a biographical drama. It tells a story of part of Booker T. Washington's life.
2. Though the text is true, it is different from facts from a book about Booker T. Washington because it tells facts about a specific time in his life in the form of a script or play. It seems more like a story rather than a list of facts about his life.

Jim Thorpe (page 101)

1. Introducing Jim Thorpe as "one of the greatest athletes of the twentieth century" is the author's way of presenting Thorpe as a person to be admired and respected for his hard work and dedication.

Answer Key *(cont.)*

2. Opening the script with a statement that Jim Thorpe is one of the greatest athletes of the twentieth century allows for the rest of the script to support this statement. Each fact stated throughout the rest of the script shows evidence of how Thorpe worked to become one of the greatest athletes.

Plant Life (page 103)

1. The line asks an important question that has to be answered by the rest of the script.
2. The author uses a script form to present facts about plant life in a way that may be more approachable and enjoyable for students.

Safety First (page 109)

1. The poet feels that safety is important and part of that is to be prepared.
2. The poem is written from a third-person point of view. You know because you don't have the words *I* or *me* in it. The word *you* is used.

Helping Hands (page 111)

1. The poem would be more personal if it were told from the first-person point of view. It would probably be about a time that someone helped the poet and gave a helping hand.
2. The poet is trying to share that people are always available to help you. The poet wants people to ask for help when they need it and use their "family and those [they] hold dear" to help them.

The Matter with Matter (page 113)

1. The use of a first-person narrative in this passage allows readers to experience the events with the speaker. It's funnier because it's told from the point of view of a person. The reader can picture the person melting and oozing.
2. The poet's point of view is to make a connection between matter and herself. She does this by describing matter first and then applying it to herself.

Who Am I (page 115)

1. The poem is more personal because it is told from the first-person point of view. It wouldn't be as impactful if it were told from the third-person point of view.
2. The speaker of this passage does not seem to be omniscient because the statements made are only from the first-person point of view.

Scene from *The Tale of Peter Rabbit* (page 121)

1. The author gives Peter Rabbit the ability to think, talk, and act like a person because it makes him more personable. The reader is more likely to form a bond or connection with Peter if he/she is able to understand his thoughts, feelings, etc.

Scene from *The Story of Doctor Dolittle* (page 123)

1. The author uses descriptive words and phrases such as "sharp horns," "very shy," and "high grass" to help illustrate the setting and animals in the passage.

Excerpt from *The Secret Garden* (page 125)

1. Imagery is used to describe the story in a way that paints a picture for the reader. Examples may include, "the earth had been turned up because a dog had scratched quite a deep hole," or "the trailing sprays of untrimmed ivy hanging from the wall."
2. By comparing the wind blowing to magic the author is instilling in the reader the notion that something out of the ordinary, fantastical, or magical is about to happen, such as a "gust of wind rush[ing] down the walk."

Excerpt from *Twenty Thousand Leagues Under the Sea* (page 127)

1. The author uses descriptive language such as: quivering, seized, glued, gasped, and choked in order to appeal to the reader's senses.
2. The violence of the scene is evident through words such as, "sweep of the ax," "fearsome tentacle," "seized by the tentacle," "glued to its suckers," and "battled with flailing axes."

Answer Key *(cont.)*

Scene from *The Adventures of Pinocchio* (page 133)

1. Some responses may include: feeling curious about where the voice is coming from; being entertained by the talking piece of wood or by the fact that the man cannot figure out where the voice is coming from; or being intrigued about who is speaking and what will happen.
2. Because Master Antonio does not know where the voice is coming from and starts to believe that he "only imagined" he heard the voice, the mysterious and curious tone of the text is much more evident.

Scene from *Mother Goose in Prose* (page 135)

1. The tone of the text is playful and adventurous. An example may include sliding down a moonbeam.
2. Based on an example such as "He decided the only way he could get there was to slide down a moonbeam," it seems that the author has a light-hearted, creative, and adventurous personality.

Excerpt from *Alice's Adventures in Wonderland* (page 137)

1. Because of the way the Hatter and the March Hare seem to not want Alice to join them at their table claiming there is "no room," it seems that the overall tone of the text is negative.
2. The dialogue contributes to the seemingly negative tone because it feels as if they are picking on Alice by saying things like, "your hair wants cutting" or "you should say what you mean."

Excerpt from *Anne of Green Gables* (page 139)

1. The reader may feel embarrassment as Anne tries to hide her green hair because she feels she is "in the depths of despair." There is also a bit of humor, however.
2. The humorous tone of the text can affect perception of the passage because it tones down the embarrassment and humiliation that Anne is feeling.

The Industrial Revolution (page 145)

1. The author uses the word *revolution* not only because it is the name of the era, but also because revolution indicates that it was a time of vast changes.
2. The sentence allows you to guess what will happen next because it hints at the fact that machines will have an affect on the way things are processed and created.

Men of the Industrial Revolution (page 147)

1. The phrase "grew and grew" refers to the notion that the company continued to expand. The next sentence also says, "his business grew."
2. The sentence reads, "At that moment, Rockefeller knew that he would go into business." It can be inferred that Rockefeller became convinced in that moment that business was what he was meant to do for a living.

European Immigration (page 149)

1. The purpose of the sentence is to transition the flow of the text from European hardships to being immigrants and not being treated very well when they first arrived in the United States.
2. Immigrants tolerated the poor working conditions because they wanted a chance at a better life in America and "did not complain. If they did not work, they had no money." They wanted to escape persecution in their home countries for having varied beliefs and values.

Asian Immigration (page 151)

1. The paragraph states that many Chinese men were able to have their family members from China join them in the United States because a large earthquake and fire destroyed all legal records including immigrants records.
2. Chinese men were willing to risk their lives to come to America because "many people were impoverished and staving" in China during the 1800s, and men wanted to be able to support their families and provide better lives for them.

Image Credits

Page	Image Description	Source
13	Oxygen atom	Teacher Created Materials
15	Water molecules	Teacher Created Materials
17	Three states of matter	Teacher Created Materials
19	Periodic Table	The Granger Collection
25	Dred Scott and his wife	The Library of Congress, Prints and Photographs Division. Washington, D.C. (LC-USZ62-79305)
27	Battle of Bull Run	The Library of Congress, Prints and Photographs Division. Washington D.C. (LC-USZC4-1796)
29	Lee signing surrender papers	The Library of Congress, Prints and Photographs Division. Washington, D.C. (LC-USZC4-1886)
37	Ancient Greek theater	Shutterstock
39	Parthenon	Shutterstock
43	Trajan's market	Corel
61	Waves	Shutterstock
63	Glasses	Shutterstock
65	Gate entrance	Shutterstock
67	Beetle	Shutterstock
85	Golden ancient castle gate	Shutterstock
87	Victorian mansion	Shutterstock
89	Baked bread	Shutterstock
91	Colonial farmhouse	Shutterstock
109	Fire engine	Shutterstock
111	Hands connected	Shutterstock
113	States of matter	Shutterstock
115	Mirror	Shutterstock
121	Peter Rabbit	Shutterstock
125	Key	Shutterstock
127	Axe	Shutterstock
133	Pinocchio puppet	Shutterstock
135	Mother Goose	Shutterstock
137	Alice in Wonderland	Shutterstock
139	Green Gables house	Shutterstock
145	Girls at the weaving machine	The Library of Congress, Prints and Photographs Division. Washington, D.C. (LC-DIG-nclc-01336)
149	Statue of Liberty	Shutterstock
151	Chinese workers canning salmon	The Library of Congress, Prints and Photographs Division. Washington, D.C. (LC-USZ62-95113)